CW00497686

Exploring Raasay

Twenty walking routes on the Isle of Raasay

With contributions from residents of Raasay
and some visitors to the island

NICK FAIRWEATHER

THIRSTY
BOOKS
EDINBURGH

First published by Thirsty Books, Edinburgh, 2015
thirstybooks.com

ISBN: 978-0-9932828-1-2

The paper used in this book is recyclable. It is made from low chlorine pulps
produced in a low energy, low emission manner from renewable forests.

Printed and bound by Bell & Bain Ltd., Glasgow

Typeset by Main Point Books, Edinburgh
mainpointbooks.co.uk

Title page photograph: Starting point for the first eight walks from the ferry terminal (TK)

CONTENTS

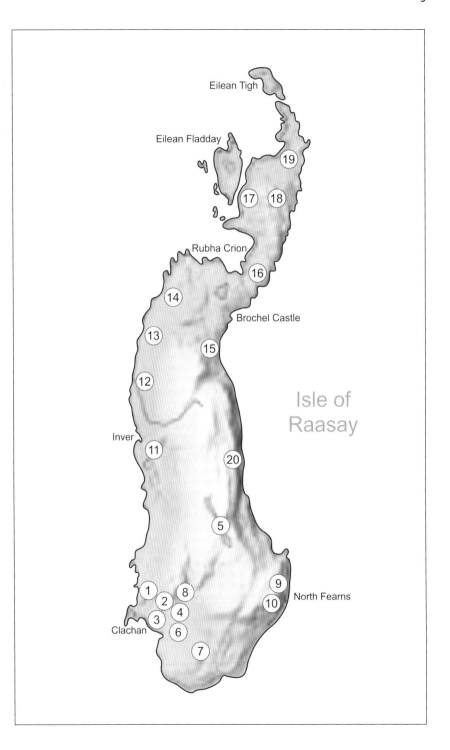

Eilean Tigh

Eilean Fladday

19

17 18

Rubha Crion

16

14

Brochel Castle

13

15

12

Isle of
Raasay

Inver

11

20

5

9

1 8

2 North Fearns

10

3 4

Clachan 6

7

Grades, Times and Maps

Each walk is graded with specific advice given about the nature of the route and it is recommended that the full description is read before starting out.

Easy: generally short and on good surfaces with some signage.

Moderate: mostly on good surfaces but some sections of rougher terrain and generally more strenuous than the easier walks. Limited signage.

Difficult: longer walks that may involve crossing rough and pathless terrain where use of a compass and a map, as a back-up for route finding, is advisable. Little or no signage.

The signs most frequently referred to in the text are shown here:

Forestry Commission

Raasay Path Network (RPN)

The times given are for round trips and are intended to be sufficiently flexible to allow for a few rest stops and some variation in fitness levels.

It is important to recognise that this is a book describing walking routes rather than way-marked footpaths. There is some signage of maintained footpaths on the island but visitors will need to find their own way on occasions using the detailed descriptions in the book.

The road to the north of the island is narrow and slow going so allow sufficient time if you are driving to the start of walks from Arnish.

The walk route maps included are based on Ordnance Survey map data for

Raasay – OS Landranger (1:50,000) Number 24. The route is shown on the map as a red line with any alternative route shown as a dotted line.

A few place names are given in both Gaelic and English but in most cases only one will be included in walk descriptions and this will be the name that is shown on Ordnance Survey maps. Visitors to the island may notice that there are some variations between the spelling of certain place names shown on Ordnance Survey maps and those used by islanders or recorded in island publications.

All of the route descriptions are linked to people who live on Raasay or visitors who have recorded their time spent on the island in some way. Thanks are due to them for their willingness to provide quotes and additional information or for taking the time to check the accuracy of route details.

Access and Safety

The ground may be wet and slippery in places so sensible footwear is advisable for all of the walks with walking boots suggested for the *Moderate* and *Difficult* graded routes. The more challenging walks offer the excitement of crossing wild country but care has to be taken, particularly if walking with children, as there are deep fissures near some of the more challenging routes and unfenced cliff edges on the coastal walks.

There can be very rapid changes in the weather so check the weather forecast and take a rucksack with waterproof and warm clothing for any of the longer walks. It may be worthwhile checking the direction of any strong winds before deciding whether to go to the west or east of the island.

Dogs have to be kept under control at all times. Raasay is a crofting community with cattle on the open hillside and widespread sheep farming. Keep dogs on leads during the spring and early summer, steering them well away from sheep and lambs. Care should be taken to avoid encroaching on fresh water supplies linked to some of the more isolated communities.

The Land Reform (Scotland) Act 2003 grants everyone the right to be on most land for recreation providing that they act responsibly. Always follow the ***Scottish Outdoor Access Code***:

• take responsibility for your own actions

• respect people's privacy and peace of mind

• help land managers and others to work safely and effectively e.g. closing gates

• care for your environment e.g. taking litter home with you, not picking wild flowers

• keep your dog under proper control.

When **parking in a lay-by** always try to leave sufficient space for its continued use as a passing place.

The author and publisher have made every effort to ensure that the information in this publication is accurate and accept no responsibility whatsoever for any loss, injury or inconvenience by any person using this book.

Acknowledgements

My thanks to all those who have contributed in some way to the preparation of this book, whether it was accompanying me on walks, advising on routes or providing background information. I am also grateful to Sean Bradley of Thirsty Books, to Raasay House and to Raasay Development Trust for making possible the publication of this book.

Many thanks are due to the seven people from the island, along with two visitors, who have contributed so much colour and interest to the book through their photographs:

Carol Anderson (CA)
David Carslaw (DC)
Margaret Ferguson (MF)
Bernie Heavey (BH)
Tekela Koek (TK)
Robin Millar (RM)
George Rankine (GR)
yAnn Rankine (yR)
Darryl Simpson (DS)

Thanks also to the artists who permitted us to reproduce their paintings:

Margaret Ferguson (MF) A local artist based in Portree whose work includes drawings, paintings, prints and tapestries: margaret.g.ferguson@gmail.com

Mairi Hedderwick (MH) Painter and writer of several books including *An Eye on the Hebrides* (Birlinn, 1989) – www.birlinn.co.uk

Lesley Skeates (LS) View a selection of her oil paintings of Scottish landscapes and seascapes at www.lesleyskeatesgallery.com

INTRODUCTION

Raasay is a special island for walkers, with forests and a rocky coastline to explore, and some of the best views available on Scotland's western seaboard from the summits of Dun Caan and neighbouring hills. Just a 25 minute boat trip from Sconser on the Isle of Skye, it offers a more intimate and varied landscape than its famous neighbour but with the panoramic backdrop of the Cuillin hills and mountain ranges on the mainland. The walking routes described in this book are full of surprises – where else could you encounter these two mammals on one walk: from the top of Dun Caan the sound of a stag roaring in Hallaig and later, back at the shore, the sight of a whale in the Sound of Raasay?

Like rings on a tree, old paths can record the evolution of an area which, once tramped, never completely disappear. You have to look hard and sometimes use a bit of imagination to find them. Many of the walks in this book reflect the changing history of the island whether it is visiting an Iron Age broch, journeying to deserted townships, following forest tracks or walking along former railways to the old iron ore mines.

The island offers opportunities for walking at all times of the year with spectacular winter views and a few of the walks easier to follow in the autumn and spring when the bracken has died back.

Whether you are coming for the day or a fortnight this book provides a variety of wonderful routes from short walks from the ferry to longer ones through some of the wilder parts of the island.

The Suisnish area in the south-west of the island with the hills of Skye in the background (CA)

Geography and Geology

Raasay, one of the Inner Hebridean Islands, is just over 14 miles long and between 2 and 3½ miles wide with a population of around 160. It lies off the east coast of Skye and is separated from Applecross, on the Scottish mainland, by the waters of the Inner Sound, one of the deepest channels around Britain. A narrow stretch of water, Caol/Kyle Rona, separates the north of Raasay from the Isle of Rona. The name 'Raasay' is commonly accepted as coming from the Norse meaning Island of the Roe Deer.

The island is of significant geological interest with a great variety of rocks on display and Raasay is visited by many geology students engaged in mapping projects. The walks have been linked (see below) to the main geological areas of the island:

The rocks of the **southern part** of the island are mainly sandstones and shales that contribute to a greener and gentler landscape. But there are two areas of granitic rocks that form Suisnish Hill, the high ground between Inverarish and Eyre, and Carn nan Eun the hillside east of Oskaig, behind the Youth Hostel, with a fault line that runs from just west of Eyre to near Oskaig.

The flat top of Dun Caan is basalt, a detached part of the lava field outpourings from the Isle of Skye volcanoes of the same Tertiary age (Walks 1 to 8).

The Jurassic sediments consisting of fossiliferous sandstones, limestones and shales are mainly found in the **east and south-east**, most notably in Hallaig Bay, the 'fossil shore'. There are also ironstones that were mined in the early twentieth century. Much of the east coast shore from Fearns to Screapadal is formed from these rocks along with the slightly older Middle Jurrasic sandstones that form the high cliffs below the summit ridge of Dun Caan (Walks 9, 10 and 20).

Raasay's **north-west**, between Inver and the road across to Brochel, is formed

mainly of Torridonian sandstone cut through by volcanic dykes creating the distinctive north-west to south-east ridges that can be followed down to visit the Manish townships and the dramatic coastline. Torridonian sandstones are the oldest sedimentary rocks in the British Isles, laid down some 1000 to 800 million years ago (Walks 11 to 14).

Gneiss rock in the north of the island (RM)

Much of the **north** of Raasay, from Brochel through Arnish and Torran up to Kyle Rona and the Isle of Rona is formed of Lewisian Gneiss, some of the oldest rocks in the world (Walks 16 to 19).

Archaeology

The first people to visit Raasay may have been Mesolithic (Middle Stone Age) travellers some 9,000 years ago, possibly on food gathering trips.

A Neolithic (new stone age) lifestyle established some 5000–6000 years ago based around a farming calendar.

An open burial cairn, constructed during the Bronze Age of 3500 years ago, can be seen close to the shore at Eyre (Walk 7). A single standing stone lies on the north side of a clearing in Church Wood.

There is an Iron Age dun, Dun Borodale, on the hill behind Inverarish (Walk 2) and underground storage chambers (souterrains), of a similar age, survive at Suisnish and opposite the Old Post Office by Raasay House.

There is a very pleasant 40 minute return walk from the telephone boxes at Inverarish to visit the Suisnish souterrain. Walk south along the road from the village and turn left after the last house in Inverarish onto a broad track that goes uphill and through two field gates. Keep on the track, past the wood-faced

Souterrain near Suisnish – photograph taken when the roof was partially uncovered (RM)

house on your right and a stone ruin and then bear right to climb up towards a mound and some more stone ruins. The fence on the top of the mound is built around the entrance to the souterrain, a roofed underground passage likely to have been used for food storage. There are splendid views of Inverarish from this mound and you can get even better ones on the way back by heading west towards the sea and climbing up onto an escarpment that you can follow back towards the wood-faced house and the track down to the road.

Pictish symbol stones can be seen at The Battery below Raasay House and by the roadside just to the north of the house (Walk 1).

There is little physical evidence of the Scandinavians settling on the island about 1100 years ago but many place names are Norse in origin – Raasay, Oskaig, Hallaig, Fladday, Holoman and Suisnish.

Towards the end of the Iron Age, Christianity replaced the old religions and Saint Moluag may have founded a chapel or cell here around 550 AD. Today this site is marked by the remains of St Moluag's Chapel, a 13th century stone building, now roofless (Walk 1).

There is limited information about the island's history during the medieval period until the MacLeods of Raasay became established at Brochel Castle in the 16th century (Walk 15).

Wildlife

Raasay has a great variety of habitats from acid moors to limestone cliffs and from coastal areas to freshwater lochs and bogs. These geological differences together with the warming effect of the Gulf Stream have created the great diversity of animal and plant life to be found on the island.

Fauna

Raasay's heather-clad moorland, forests and sea cliffs are home to some 60 species of birds including golden eagle, sea eagle, sparrow hawk, tawny owl, spotted and pied flycatcher and redstart.

On the moors and open country you may see golden plovers, and ring ouzels are also regular visitors. In summer the sheltered bays, sandy inlets and foreshore are alive to the call of nesting waders, oystercatchers, sandpipers and curlews. Golden eagles nest on the island and sea eagles are frequent visitors. Red-throated divers nest by several lochs and great northern divers visit during the winter – though in recent years they have stayed into spring and early summer.

There are at least 250 red deer on the island and Raasay has its own unique sub-species of bank vole, darker and twice the weight of the mainland vole. The inshore waters with their abundance of shellfish and the freshwater streams and lochs provide an island 'playground' for otters.

Dolphin in Churchton Bay (GR)

Basking sharks can be seen in the waters around the island, also Minke whales and Orca. There are regular sightings of schools of dolphins and porpoises just offshore, and grey seals breed and raise their pups in the inner and outer sounds, the stretches of water between the islands and the Scottish mainland.

Flora

The island is extremely rich in flora too with over 600 species of flowering plants and ferns recorded in recent years. There are plants of highly contrasting

Orchid (TK)

geographical distribution within Europe, and several nationally scarce or threatened species. There are about 40 different native ferns and fern allies found on Raasay, from the aptly named small adder's-tongue to bracken, great horsetail and royal fern.

Many different orchids grow and, in some cases, hybridise. Bird's-nest orchid has not been seen for many years but the rare Lapland marsh orchid has a strong presence in one area. The limestone cliffs on the east side of the island are home to many ferns and flowering plants including holly fern, dark-red helleborine and mountain avens as well as many more common plants such as wild thyme, wall-rue and fairy flax.

(*Based on information provided by Raasay House.*)

Some key dates in the history of Raasay

In the early 16th century the island of Raasay was bestowed by Calum MacLeod, the ninth chief of Lewis, on his younger son Calum Garbh, the first chief of the MacLeods of Raasay based at Brochel Castle.

1671   The MacLeod's chiefs left Brochel Castle and moved to Clachan in the south of the island.

1746   After Culloden the clan house at Clachan was burnt to the ground and 300 homes destroyed by government troops as reprisal for MacLeod's support for the uprising. Prince Charles Edward Stuart sheltered in Raasay for two days before returning to Skye and making his way back to France.

1773   Samuel Johnson and James Boswell made their journey to the Western Isles and were entertained as guests of the MacLeod chief in the recently rebuilt Raasay House.

1809   The Battery, the fortified mound just behind the ferry terminal, was constructed to counter a threatened invasion by France.

1824   The financial problems of the MacLeod lairds increased due to massive expenditure on the development of the house and estate. Some tenant farmers emigrated as rents increased and sheep farming was introduced.

1843   The last laird, John MacLeod, emigrated with his family to Australia.

1846   Raasay Estate was sold to George Rainy when the population of the island was over 1000.

1852–4   Over 150 people emigrated from Fearns, Leac and Hallaig with the assistance of the Highlands and Islands Emigration Society. Shortly after this the remaining scattered population were evicted to make way for sheep farming.

1861   The Census shows that the majority of the island's population was now crowded into the north of Raasay or living on Rona.

1872–6   The estate changed hands three times before being sold to Edward Herbert Wood, an industrial magnate who created a sporting estate and added the ornate Georgian-style wings and frontage to Raasay House.

1883   Evidence to the Napier Commission, the Royal Commission inquiry into the conditions of crofters and cottars in the Highlands and Islands, detailed the hardships experienced by the islanders forced to live in the north of the island and on Rona.

1911   Wm Baird & Co., Ironmasters bought the estate and operated an iron ore mine on the island until 1920 by which time the price of ore dropped from 6 shillings to 4 pence per ton making the mines unprofitable.

1921   A group of men from Rona, who became known as the 'Raasay Raiders', seized land in Fearns after repeatedly applying to the land owner and the Board of Agriculture for Scotland to be resettled in the more fertile land at the south end of the island.

1922   The then Board of Agriculture purchased the island from Bairds for £18,000 and a year later took over managing the estate to resettle crofters and cottars.

1961   Raasay House was purchased for £6,000 by Dr Green from Sussex.

1964   After several years campaigning for the council to build a road from Brochel to his home in Arnish, Calum MacLeod decided to start building one himself. He completed his single-handed construction of a one and three quarter mile road in 1974.

1979   Highlands and Islands Development Board (subsequently Highlands and Islands Enterprise) purchased Raasay House and other properties on the island.

1981   The Scottish Adventure School Trust established and when this closed two years later the Raasay Outdoor Centre Ltd was set up.

2007   Raasay House Community Company formed under the Land Reform Act to purchase Raasay House, its walled garden, the policies and associated woodlands from Highlands and Islands Enterprise, on behalf of the island community.

AIRD GHIUTHAIS/ ARDHUISH AND CAMUS ALBA/ NORTH BAY

This short walk provides an excellent introduction to the Isle of Raasay's beautiful coastline with magnificent views across to Skye.

Route

1. From the ferry slipway walk to the left of the ferry terminal building and around the back of the mound known as The Battery, complete with a cannon on top to counter a rumoured French invasion in the early 19th century. You will probably also have spotted the two stone mermaids which were designed for the balcony of Raasay House. They were too heavy – as was their cost, which contributed to the financial ruin of the last laird of Raasay, John MacLeod, resulting in the sale of the island and considerable hardship for much of the island population.

START/ FINISH
Ferry terminal car park

DISTANCE
3K/ 2 miles

TIME
1 to 1½ hours

GRADE/ ADVICE
Easy. Sensible footwear advisable as the path may be eroded in places and slippery when wet.

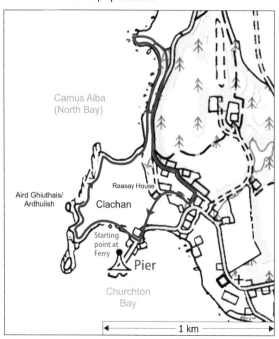

Ardhuish headland with Ben
Tianavaig in background (TK)

2. Head towards a wooden Raasay Path Network
(RPN) sign and follow a path line in the grass
keeping to the left of the fence around the harbour.
Go through the wooden gate and turn left along a
narrow path, eroded in places, that climbs up to
the Ardhuish headland. There are now magnificent
views across the Sound of Raasay, back to the
Cuillins and northwards to the hills of Trotternish.
You will pass a further four wooden marker posts
before entering a 'tunnel' of rhododendrons. This
section could be muddy and care needs to be taken
when walking across the plant roots on the path.

3. Pass through the iron gate, signposted
'Launderette', and walk on the grassy track to your
right alongside the fence.

4. Follow the next wooden footpath sign which
points down to your left and walk along the
shoreline of Camas Alba/ North Bay. It is eroded
in parts but it is a beautiful bay and there is the

possibility of seeing an otter searching for food at the water's edge. Continue along this path, to the end of the curve in the bay, ignoring an RPN sign, next to a ruin, pointing to the right, to climb up on to a small headland There are good views up and down the Sound of Raasay and over to Skye.

The path alongside Camas Alba/ North Bay (DS)

5. Walk away from the sea towards the path alongside the stone wall at the edge of the forest.

6. After a few minutes, and at the next wooden signpost (pointing straight ahead), bear right taking the path into the forest and follow this until reaching the road. (The signposted path takes you on to the longer walk of Churchton Bay and Raasay Woods – see Walk 4.)

On the road back towards Raasay House (RM)

St Moluag's Chapel (CA)

7. Turn right onto the tarmac and follow the fine stretch of road along a terrace with views down to the sea on your right. After about half a mile the road bends to the left to go around the sides of the walled garden of Raasay House, passing the cemetery of the MacLeods. This contains two buildings, the 12th or 13th century St Moluag's Chapel and a more recent memorial chapel, unroofed, built by the last of the MacLeod lairds in memory of his daughter who died aged three.

Raasay House (CA)

8. Continue along the road for another 200 metres before reaching the entrance to Raasay House. A clan house, home to the MacLeods of Raasay, has stood on or near to this site since the 1600s. The current building, which dates back to 1747, was where the laird entertained Samuel Johnson and James Boswell. The ornate Georgian style wings and frontage were added in the 1870s and the house is now an outdoor centre and hotel with a bar and restaurant. A very good place to end a walk.

Additional information kindly provided by Moira and Bob Williams who have a house on the island.

TEMPTATION HILL

A walk for all seasons and weathers that takes you to a grand viewpoint overlooking the Sound of Raasay. The route passes a secluded loch in the woods and offers the chance to explore an Iron Age broch.

Route

1. Walk up the road from the ferry terminal until you see the sign for Raasay House. Follow the track between the fields, through the gate and around the left side of the house to the back entrance and turn left onto the tarmac road. Look out for the Pictish symbol stone situated beside the road on your right in a small clearing amongst the trees. About 30 metres from here you will see a signpost to Temptation Hill pointing uphill to your right (Forest Trails and the Raasay Path Network [RPN] signs).

2. Follow this clearly defined path through the forest as it zigzags uphill, with steps and a handrail at the steepest section. As you get to the highest point there is a short rocky path on your left which takes you even higher, up to the top of Temptation Hill. It is a magnificent view across the Sound, and there is

START/ FINISH
Ferry terminal car park

DISTANCE
5K/ 3 miles

TIME
1½ to 2 hours

HIGHEST POINT
99 metres

GRADE/ ADVICE
Easy. The route is quite steep and narrow in a couple of places and may be slippery when wet, but mostly on good paths, tracks or tarmac.

The Pictish symbol stone (RM)

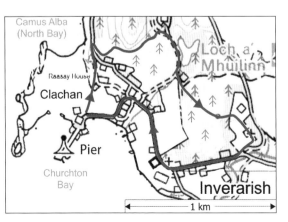

a seat to give you time to enjoy it and maybe watch the progress of a ferry crossing to and from Sconser. There are various reasons given for use of the name 'Temptation' including the smell of roasting pig, someone tempted to become the proprietor of the island, and an Austrian lady who came to Raasay and was tempted back. Maybe, as one islander told me, the simple reason is that it was a place that local courting couples enjoyed visiting! The memorial stone to Kit, a 19 year old girl who died of the fever, was erected by her fiancé and refers to Raasay as 'an earthly paradise as it is like heaven to me'.

The view from the top of Temptation Hill (DC)

3. Return to the main footpath, which leads downhill at first, to the edge of the woodland. It can be slippery when wet but it is stepped and railed for part of the way. The grassy footpath is easy to follow around the edge of the cleared ground on your right, with panoramic views across Borodale Park to Skye.

4. There are more footpath signs and a Forestry Commission information board once you reach a levelled stony gravel area and come to a tarmac road. The route continues to the right and you can

Neolithic dolmen burial site (RM)

either walk down the road to reach the corner of Loch a' Mhuilinn, also referred to as the Home Loch, or follow a footpath through the forest which runs parallel to the tarmac option. The latter is more enjoyable, if a bit more confusing as you encounter a maze of footpaths, but if you always choose the left hand fork then you can't go too far wrong. As you walk through the trees you may see to your right a massive flat rock perched precariously on some smaller stones. This is a Neolithic dolmen or cromlech, a 5000 year old burial site.

You will shortly reach a track on your left which takes you out onto the tarmac road. Turn left and walk uphill for about 100 metres to reach Loch a' Mhuilinn which is surrounded by rhododendrons and looks stunning when in full bloom during May/ June. Several herons nest here each year, in the trees on the far side of the loch.

(If you have had enough walking by this stage you can take a shortcut by continuing down the road, turning right at a junction near some houses and onto the 'main' road that leads down to the ferry terminal.)

5. There is an RPN sign just by Loch a' Mhuilinn indicating a short path that leads around the edge of the loch, passing a picnic table and joining up with a broad track. Follow this track uphill through the pine forest and then bear right at the next junction, signed as the 'Temptation Hill Trail'.

6. Just after reaching the edge of the forest you can take a detour, signed on your right, to visit the site of Dun Bhorghadail/ Dun Borodale, an Iron Age broch, a short climb uphill from the main path. This is a fortified oval-shaped dwelling that would have

Loch a' Mhuilinn (DC)

been occupied by the Picts about 2000 years ago, and although much of the stone has been removed it is still an imposing structure due, in part, to its commanding location.

7. Back on the main track follow the RPN signs downhill, keeping the large house, the Manse, to your left and, a little further on, passing the Free Church of Scotland. Continue on the path downhill through the rhododendron bushes to arrive at a road junction. The village of Inverarish, with the island's community shop, can be reached by turning left and then first right after crossing the bridge. Alternatively turn right and follow the road for the 1½ kilometres back towards Raasay House and the ferry.

Additional information kindly provided by Tekela Koek, a keen walker who lives on the island.

SHORE PATH TO INVERARISH AND THE EMIGRANTS' WALK

START/ FINISH
Ferry terminal

DISTANCE
4K/ 2½ miles

TIME
1 hour

If the detour to Suisnish point is included add 3K/ 2 miles and 40 minutes to above estimates.

GRADE/ ADVICE
Easy. Short sections of the shore path and through the forest may be a bit boggy so boots or sensible shoes advisable.

If you want to avoid all rough ground you can follow a triangular route along the roads to and from Inverarish.

Follow the shore path to Inverarish, the largest village on the island, and return along the Emigrants' Walk and through woodland to Clachan and the ferry.

Route

1. From the ferry terminal walk round the bay and after 200 metres turn right to follow a short tarmac road down and then uphill towards a wooden gate. Bear right just before this and walk down the gravel path (with hand rail) and then up steps, past the entrance to a private house, to a metal kissing gate.

2. Enter the field and turn right to walk along the edge for about 100 metres before going through another kissing gate. You might get stared at by some friendly cattle but as long as you keep to the edge of the field they won't bother you.

3. There is now a clear path alongside a boundary wall on your right with great views across the Sound of Raasay towards the Cuillins on Skye. This path has been here for at least a hundred years and

Churchton Bay at the start of
Walk 3 (NF)

was used as a shortcut by the village people when collecting their milk from the dairy at Clachan.

4. Pass through another kissing gate and out on to open ground then down through a copse of alder trees. After going through the fourth gate follow the path that loops to the left around a small fenced off area to reach the track along the front of the Community Hall and on to a tarmac road. (This will be 15 to 20 minutes walk from the ferry.)

5. Turn right at the road and walk downhill, past the playing fields near the shore and the planned Heritage Centre building on your left before crossing a bridge over the Inverarish Burn.

6. If you have time you might want to take a 40 minute detour at this T-junction, to walk along the coast road to Suisnish Point and back. This headland is indicated by a tall yellow cable marker post just after a picnic table. There are fine views over to Skye and, if you are lucky, a chance to see an otter feeding in the kelp and rocks at the water's edge.

This road also gives access to the souterrain, an Iron Age narrow underground passage that was used for cold storage, which is up a track behind Suisnish –

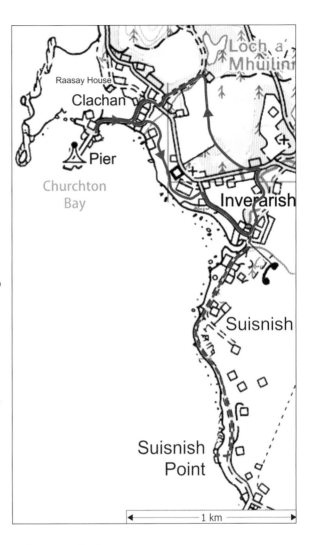

The road from the Community
Hall down towards Inverarish and
Suisnish (DC)

see the section on archaeology in the Introduction
for more details.

7. A left turn at the junction takes you to the village
of Inverarish where former miners cottages are laid
out in two parallel terraces either side of a strip
of garden greenery (and numerous sheds). The
community-owned shop is at the top end of the
terrace and there are picnic tables here and also
down in the car park on your left.

8. Now follow the 'Emigrants Walk'/ 'Ceum nan
Eilthireach', which starts from the tarmac car park
and follows a delightful trail through the woods
alongside the Inverarish Burn as it flows between
two former mills – the meal mill at Inverarish and
the nearby sawmill. The trail has been laid out to
remember the many people from Raasay who,
forced by politics, poverty and landlords, emigrated
overseas between 1720 and 1884. There is a series
of commemorative plaques along the way that
chart the travels of these pioneering people to
the West Indies, America, Canada, New Zealand
and Australia. Native plants from these countries

including eucalyptus, olearia, sugar maples and dogwood have been planted near the appropriate plaque.

The village of Inverarish looking from the Fire Station up towards the community shop (RN)

9. Turn left onto the road at the end of the Emigrants' Walk, passing the sawmill in the woods, and after about 200 metres you will come to a small grassy clearing on your right, just after the 30 mph speed limit sign. At this point you can continue along the road all the way to the ferry but a more interesting option is to look for the small gap in the rhododendron bushes across to your right and find the narrow pine needle covered path that climbs up into the forest.

10. Keep climbing up the main path, ignoring narrower side routes, to emerge from the forest at an old stone wall where you can enjoy a fine view across the field down to the ferry harbour and beyond to the Trotternish hills on Skye. Follow the path that runs between the stone wall and the edge of the pine forest passing some fine examples of ancient larch and Scots pine. The path broadens into

One of the bridges across the Inverarish Burn on the Emigrants' Walk (CA)

An otter at the shoreline (GR)

a track and goes downhill to reach a rough tarmac road some 15 minutes after you entered the forest.

11. Turn left and walk down this track, past the 'Old Post Office' house to reach the main island road where you can turn right for the short walk down to the ferry terminal, or maybe pay a visit to Raasay House for some refreshment.

Additional information kindly provided by Ann and Donnie Oliphant, the owners of those cows and the croft that Ann inherited from her grandfather, the shoemaker at Clachan.

CHURCHTON BAY AND RAASAY WOODS

With fabulous coastal scenery and atmospheric woodlands, this is one of the classic routes on the island, combining Walks 1 and 2 into a half-day outing. It appears in several publications including *The Scotsman* where columnist Robin Howie described Raasay in his 'Walk of the Week', as 'the earthly paradise because it's like heaven to me', quoting from the memorial stone on Temptation Hill.

Route

1 From the ferry slipway walk to the left of the ferry terminal building and around the back of the grassy mound with its two large stone sculptures of mermaids. These were erected by the last MacLeod owner of Raasay House and their cost contributed to his financial downfall and the sale of the island.

2. Head towards a wooden Raasay Path Network (RPN) walks sign and follow a path line in the grass keeping to the left of the fence around the harbour. Go through the wooden gate and turn left along a narrow path, eroded in places, that climbs up to the Ardhuish headland. There are now magnificent views across the Sound of Raasay, back to the Cuillins and northwards to the hills of Trotternish. You will pass four more wooden marker posts before entering a 'tunnel' of rhododendrons. This section could be muddy

START/ FINISH
Ferry terminal car park

DISTANCE
7K/ 4½ miles

TIME
3 to 4 hours

GRADE/ ADVICE
Easy. Well signed but sensible footwear advisable as the path may be eroded in places and slippery when wet.

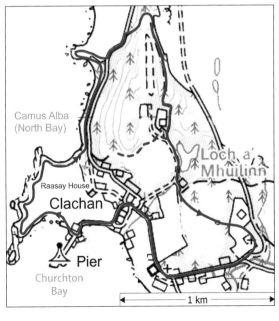

Camus Alba
(North Bay)

Loch a' Mhuilinn

Raasay House

Clachan

Pier

Churchton Bay

1 km

The beach at the south end of
Camas Alba/ North Bay (DS)

and care needs to be taken when walking across
the plant roots on the path.

3. Pass through the iron gate, signed 'Launderette',
and walk on the grassy track to your right alongside
the fence.

4. The next wooden footpath sign points down
to your left to walk along the shoreline of North
Bay. Continue along this path, eroded in parts, and
round the curve at the end of the bay, ignoring an
RPN sign, next to a ruin, pointing to the right, to
climb up on to a small headland There are good
views up and down the Sound of Raasay and over
to Skye.

5. Walk away from the sea towards the path
alongside the stone wall at the edge of the forest
and up to a metal gate. Turn left and walk along the
road for 100 metres or so and then go through the
metal gate on your right to follow the RPN 'Orchard
Path' sign uphill to a stand of Scots Pines. Keep
following the path as it bears right to enter a pass

between the rocky escarpment on your left and the forest on your right. You can still see evidence of the storm damage when a gale force wind from the north swept through this valley and felled part of the forest overnight.

6. When you reach the high stone wall that encloses the old orchard of Raasay House, turn left and then right to walk along the side of it to join a rough tarmac road. You can now make a detour to visit Temptation Hill by turning right across a cleared area of gravel and following signs along a grassy path above an area of felled forest to reach some steep steps that take you up to this viewpoint. (See Walk 2 for more details.)

7. To continue the walk follow the road downhill to the edge of Loch a' Mhuilinn, sometimes referred to as the Home Loch. There is an RPN sign indicating a short path through rhododendrons around the edge of the loch, passing a picnic table at the lochside,

Looking south towards Skye from near the north end of Camas Alba/ North Bay (TK)

Looking south-east along the track heading towards the Free Church of Scotland in Borodale Wood (CA)

which joins up with a broad track. Turning left, take this route uphill through the pine forest and then bear right at the next junction, signed as the 'Temptation Hill Trail'.

8. Just after reaching the edge of the forest there is a short detour, on the right, which you can take to visit the site of Dun Bhorghadail/ Dun Borodale, an ancient broch some 200 metres uphill from the main path. This is a fortified oval-shaped dwelling which would have been occupied by the Picts about 2000 years ago and although much of the stone has been removed, it is still an imposing structure due, in part, to its commanding location.

9. Back on the main track follow the RPN signs downhill, past the large house on your left and then, on your right, the Free Church of Scotland. The path continues downhill through the rhododendron bushes to arrive at a road junction. The village of Inverarish is just 400 metres to your left if you want to visit the island's community shop; otherwise turn right and follow the road for the 1½ kilometres back towards Raasay House and the ferry.

Additional information kindly provided by Robin Howie whose weekly column, 'Walk of the Week', appears in The Scotsman *each Saturday. Author of* 100 Scotsman Walks, *Robin's name is very well-known in hillwalking circles.*

DUN CAAN – TWO ROUTES

A climb from the ferry terminal up to the dramatic basalt plug summit of Dun Caan, the highest peak on the island. The view from the summit is one of the finest on Scotland's western seaboard and was used in the opening sequence of the BBC's 'Men of Rock' series about Scottish geologists. As its presenter, Iain Stewart, says: 'What a view. This is our ancient heritage laid out before our very eyes.'

Route from the ferry

1. Walk up the path alongside the road from the ferry terminal, turn right at the steading building with the clock tower and then almost immediately left at the next tarmac track, signposted as the 'Orchard Path', alongside a small white building used, at the time of writing, by a jewellery business, The Silver Grasshopper.

2. Walk up the track for about 300 metres and turn right along a narrow path by the loch for about 50 metres and then go left onto a wide track into the forest.

3. In 200 metres take the left fork onto a slightly narrower track and when you reach a road follow the path on the other side which is signed with a green footpath marker. This path climbs up through the forest, crosses a small clearing full of rhododendrons and then goes through an iron gate and down along a grand avenue of trees.

4. Keep to the left at the next clearing, beside the footpath marker, and along a narrow path which emerges from the forest onto a broad track. Turn left onto this and head up and around the top of the

START/ FINISH

Start and finish at the ferry terminal for the main walk. If you have transport and want a shorter outing you could climb Dun Caan from Balmeanach which is about a 5 mile drive from the ferry.

DISTANCE

From/to ferry:
14.5K/ 9 miles

From/to Balmeanach:
6K/ 4 miles

TIME

5 to 6 hours
2½ to 3 hours

GRADE/ ADVICE

Difficult. Moderate.

Both routes require care when climbing up and down some steep rocky paths near the summit but despite this the shorter route is still considered to be moderately easy. The longer route is classified as difficult given that it is over rougher terrain, with care needed to keep on the right path. It can be wet underfoot and may require a bit of hopping to avoid the boggiest sections.

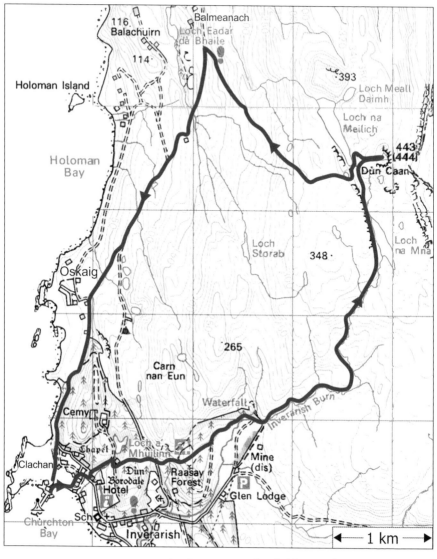

glen to cross two footbridges and arrive at a path junction and a sign for Dun Caan (3.8K).

5. Take the narrow rocky path from the green marker post to climb up to the left of the Inverarish Burn and waterfalls, particularly impressive after heavy rains, to reach a well sprung wood and metal gate. Go through this gate and follow the path, initially alongside the deer fence (don't cross the stile), and

then use the Inverarish Burn as your main guide for
the next 2½ kilometres, crossing the moorland up to
Loch na Mna, below the summit crags of Dun Caan.
It is a very pleasant walk alongside the tumbling burn
as it winds its way across the moor, although the path
is indistinct and wet in places. About halfway to Loch
na Mna the route moves away from the burn to cut
a corner and you gain enough height to spot, in the
distance, the top of Dun Caan.

The path through the
woods at the start of
the longer walk to
Dun Caan (RM)

Painting of the route to Dun Caan, looking back down Inverarish Burn (LS)

6. The next section can be particularly wet after heavy rains but then the path begins to climb up towards the last fence post on the horizon and reach the high point on the ridge with a large cairn and a clear view across to your hill. Cross the low stile just after this and head for the shores of Loch na Mna and the ramparts of Dun Caan. As you near the water's edge you have a choice of following a path that goes up onto the escarpment ahead or bearing to your right to walk along the rocky shore of the loch, the home, according to legend, of a wild sea horse which devoured a blacksmith's daughter. The father then roasted a sow at the edge

of the loch to tempt the monster and slew the beast when it came on land.

7. The route along the water's edge is more direct and once you have negotiated the rocks at the end of the loch you can follow the faint path which begins to head up the grassy slope to the left of Dun Caan's summit ridge. As you continue to climb you will begin to see another loch, Loch na Meilich, down on your left and you will soon meet up with the main path that zigzags up from there to the summit of Dun Caan. Turn onto this path to head uphill and round to the rocky but easy ridge up the north of the hill to reach the OS pillar at the top, some 2¾ hours after leaving the ferry. If the weather is clear you may want to spend time picking out the hills and islands all around, from Kintail to the Outer Hebrides, from Torridon and Applecross to the Cuillin and Trotternish ridges on Skye. No wonder the Druids celebrated here, and James Boswell danced a jig.

8. The return route starts from near the OS pillar and back down the zigzag path, this time staying on it all the way to the shores of Loch na Meilich. Cross the head of the loch and climb up the path diagonally ascending the rocky escarpment on the far side to reach a lochan on top of this small plateau. There is now a good track at an easy angle, initially going west and then north-west all the way down to the

View of the summit of Dun Caan across the waters of Loch na Mna (RM)

road at Balmeanach. If walking on your own, this may be the time to listen to music or, in company, an opportunity to put the world to rights. There is plenty to look at from the striking shape of Holoman Island, the white houses near Balmeanach and across the Sound of Raasay to Ben Tianavaig and the bay at Portree.

9. When you reach the road turn left to head south and follow it down to a gully before climbing up and passing the island's water works. Keep going straight ahead at the next road junction, signed to Inverarish, and approximately 2½ kilometres and some 25 minutes after joining the road, go through a metal field gate on your right, and walk along the gravel track to a metal kissing gate. There are fine views across the green fields of Oskaig and over to Skye as you walk down a short grassy track to join the road heading south for the ferry.

This is a beautiful stretch of road, past the houses and fields of Oskaig, through a wood and along a terrace above the waters of North Bay. In the

Sound of Raasay you can often see small boats from Portree on wildlife trips looking for sea eagles at the base of the cliffs of Ben Tianavaig, or coming nearer to the Raasay shoreline to watch seals off Holoman Island. If you have binoculars it may be worth taking a closer look to see what they have spotted because it might just be a whale or a group of dolphins or porpoises.

10. Just after passing a Pictish symbol stone on your left, dating from about 1000 AD, you will arrive at the back entrance of Raasay House and you can take this shortcut to the ferry, or perhaps visit the bar or restaurant for some refreshment.

A winter's view of the Cuillin hills on Skye from the top of Dun Caan (RM)

Short route from Balmeanach

The iron gate on the Dun Caan route heading down to Oskaig (NF)

1. Drive from the ferry terminal to Balmeanach where there is ample parking space in a large lay-by beside a picnic table. The signposted track (Dun Caan 2.9K) climbs up the hillside at an easy angle and, although you can't see the summit at this stage, the route up to a small lochan is straightforward.

2. You now have a good view across to the summit of Dun Caan and whilst, at first glance, the paths down the rocky escarpment and up to the summit look rather daunting, the angles of the slopes are easier than they look.

3. Follow the rocky path down to Loch na Meilich, walk along the shore at the end of the loch and up a clear path that zigzags its way firstly to the north of the hill and then through the rocks and up to the summit.

4. Retrace your steps to return to the starting point at Balmeanach.

The quote is kindly provided by Iain Stewart, Professor of Geosciences Communication at Plymouth University and presenter of the Men of Rock *BBC series which retraces the steps of scientists working in Scotland who pioneered geological study and understanding.*

THE MINERS' TRAIL – RAASAY'S IRON ORE MINES

This is a chance to learn more about the iron ore mining on the island and enjoy a forest walk. The second part of the route is across open moorland, with the Cuillin hills of Skye as a backdrop, and back along the coast road to the former mining village of Inverarish.

Route

1. Walk along the main road from the ferry, turning right at the low steading building (with clock tower) and bear left at the next road junction after the church. After approximately ½ kilometre take a left turn up the tarmac road and 300 metres later turn right into the Forestry Commission car park.

2. There is a useful Forestry Commission Information Board in the car park about mining during the First World War on Raasay. The buildings of the second of the two underground mines on the island are on your left – a 'fan house' for mine ventilation and the 'hauler house' for operation of the cable for the railway. The discovery of serious

START/ FINISH

If you have transport then you may prefer to start and finish this walk from stage 2 at the Forestry Commission car park in the woods or the car parking spaces next to the mine number 1 buildings at stage 5. Alternatively, start/ finish at the ferry terminal and walk along the road, as described in the first stage of the route below.

DISTANCE

7K/ 4½ miles

TIME

3 to 4 hours

GRADE/ ADVICE

Easy. Well signed.

Artist's impression of the iron ore mining tunnel (MF)

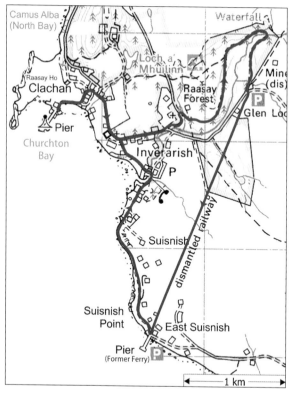

geological faults meant that this No. 2 mine never fully operated and the entrance to the mine has collapsed. You can just see, to your right, the piers of the railway viaduct that was intended to carry the cable-hauled trucks on tracks to and from Suisnish Pier.

3. Walk across the car park to your right to find a narrow path that goes up over a small mound, past a rectangular stone building where they kept the explosives for the mine, and into the forest on a broad track referred to as the 'Burma Road'. This was built by forestry workers in the 1950s as a route to the sawmill near Inverarish.

4. After about 10 minutes you will reach the high point of the track and emerge from the trees onto

Entrance to Number One mine (NF)

a broad grassy path that goes along the edge of the forest for over ½ kilometre. You can now see some of the mine buildings to your right on the other side of the Inverarish Burn, and the walk will make its way towards these around the head of the glen. Continue on the path as it curves round to the right and crosses the Inverarish Burn, with a fine view, particularly after heavy rain, of a waterfall on your left. Now walk along the gravel road to reach the No. 1 mine buildings, approximately 40 minutes after leaving the car park.

5. There is another helpful information board here briefly describing the work of the miners in drilling and blasting iron ore from a 5 mile network of underground tunnels. The actual entrance to the mine is hidden in undergrowth to the left, at the back of the buildings. There is a path that leads to a stone-sided water channel and you can just

Miner's Trail walking route alongside the pillars of the railway viaduct (MF)

see, through the trees, the metal grille which blocks up the entrance to the mine. There is not much more to see if you attempt to cross this water channel; with the stones often slippery, it is not advisable to go any further. The 'hauler house' and 'compressor house' buildings are the larger buildings with the intriguingly named 'counting house' at the back. The third area of mining on the island was an open cast mine further up the hillside behind these buildings, near to the road over to Fearns.

6. Now cross the main road and follow signs to the (former) Ferry Pier (2.5K) and the Miners' Trail (1.4K).

View over to Inverarish from the Miner's Trail route (DC)

You are now walking along the line of the cable railway heading towards the south of the island with magnificent views across to the Cuillin hills on Skye. After passing through a gate, follow a line of low birch trees to reach the edge of a gorge. With only the pillars of the railway viaduct remaining you have to follow a stepped path on your left down to the burn – easy to cross in summer months but less so if there have been heavy winter rains. Once on the other side, follow a path through the grass up to a Raasay Paths Network (RPN) sign.

7. There is a shortcut here to the right, signed as the Miners' Trail, and in 10 minutes this will take you back to the road near Inverarish. This path crosses grassy moorland and down to a cutting for the railway track from the No. 2 Mine to Suisnish. Turn right onto this broad grassy track and into the wooded area where you have to scramble down a path on your left to avoid reaching a dead end at the side walls of the viaduct. Turn left onto the road and follow this to the junction near Inverarish. Turn left again if you want to visit the village shop, or continue straight ahead across the bridge and either turn right at the next junction to return to the car park, or continue on the road back to the ferry.

8. To stay on the main walk continue going straight ahead, signed to the old Ferry Pier at Suisnish, towards a line of trees and a broad grassy track through the heather. Just after going through another gate you arrive at the junction of the railway lines from the two mines and a stone built 'hauler house' building.

9. The grassy track across the moor is clear to see and after another 10 minutes you will arrive at a cutting through the rock and then look down the steep slope to the pier and the iron ore processing plant buildings. The ore was crushed and then heated in large kilns but the top towers of these ovens have been removed and all you can now see are the five bases on the left, looking rather like a row of small sad houses. The giant concrete hopper remains as does the shell of the low administration building down on the right but all of the ironwork has been removed and there is no evidence of the conveyor belts used to carry the processed ore across to the pier head and onto the waiting ships.

10. Turn right onto the road for the 20 minute walk back to Inverarish along the coast with maybe a chance of spotting an otter at the water's edge.

The old pier head at the end of
the railway (CA)

The first double terrace of houses in the village
of Inverarish was built to house miners from as
far afield as Italy and Belgium, with more homes
added later to accommodate prisoners of war.
The community-owned shop is on the main road
at the top of the village. To return to your starting
point, walk up the road past the shop and turn left
at the first road junction to cross over Henderson
Bridge. The car park is about 300 metres up the
first turning on the right after the bridge. If walking
to the ferry, continue straight on along the road to
reach the terminal in about 10 minutes.

*Additional information and checking of this route kindly
provided by Ann and Sandy MacLeod who live on the
island.*

SUISNISH HILL PATH TO EYRE POINT AND RETURN VIA FEARNS

A fine walk across the high ground between Inverarish and Eyre with views across to Scalpay and Skye from the top of Suisnish Hill. The return route follows the shoreline to Fearns and then back along the road to the ferry.

Route

1. Walk along the main road from the ferry, turning right at the low steading building (with clock tower) and then bear left at the next road junction after the church. Continue along the road for 800 metres crossing Henderson Bridge and going straight ahead, signposted 'Fearns' (so not the 'North Pole') at the junction until you see, just as you reach the large concrete pillars of the mining railway viaduct, signs for the Miners' Trail on your right. Follow the start of this signposted trail, climbing steeply up the side of the pillar and then walk along the path between the line of trees and out onto the open hillside.

2. Follow this straight track, the line of the old mining railway, for a short distance, bearing left at the Raasay Paths Network (RPN) sign to take a path through felled woodland and arrive, in just over 5 minutes, at a path junction. Ignore the sign to the left for the Miners' Trail and go straight ahead onto a narrow and, initially, rather indistinct path through the grass. It becomes more obvious as you walk through another area of felled forest, climbing gradually up to a wooden stile. Cross over the stile and take the path that heads in a south-easterly direction, initially aiming just to the left of the highest point on the horizon ahead of you.

START/ FINISH
The ferry terminal

DISTANCE
15K/ 9¼ miles

TIME
4 to 5 hours

HIGHEST POINT
141 metres

GRADE/ ADVICE
Moderate. Mostly easy walking, although muddy in places, but classed as moderate because careful navigation is required to find the route down to the road at Eyre, particularly in summer when the bracken is high.

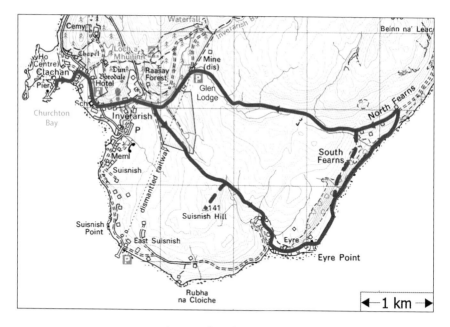

3. Just after dropping down to cross a burn the path forks and you take the right hand one, marked with a small cairn, and the route flattens out to contour around the hillside. The path then bends sharply to the left just before you reach the brow, with views to the east over to the distant hills of Kintail and, to the south, the neighbouring island of Scalpay. Some 25 metres further on, at a small cairn, there is a faint path on your right through grass and heather heading south and uphill towards the summit of Suisnish Hill. There are little more than animal tracks to follow but it is a short 10 minute walk across some undulating ground on the way up to the OS pillar. It is worth the effort, to enjoy the views across the south of Raasay and over the water to Skye and Scalpay.

4. Retrace your steps northwards from the summit, back to the main path and follow this down the gully to cross a burn, then up and along the ridge on the other side. The path goes south-east to begin with and then more southerly, heading towards a small beach in the distance near Eyre. The route follows

the line of a low stone wall on your right and when this turns across your path to head uphill, you can make your way through a small gap.

5. Shortly after crossing the wall you arrive at a barbed wire fence with a small iron gate straight ahead of you, and a larger metal field gate on your right. Go through the field gate making sure to close it behind you, and enter the enclosure around some substantial ruined buildings just ahead. There are several houses spread over this hillside including one, slightly further to the east, that was the former family home of the famous MacKay pipers. In the early 19th century John MacKay was piper to the laird. One of his sons, Angus, became piper to Queen Victoria and was responsible for writing down for publication, for the first time ever, a wealth of pipe music, helping to establish the bagpipe's role in highland culture.

View across to Skye from the route over Suisnish Hill (RM)

The beach at Eyre at the south end of Raasay (RM)

6. This is now the challenging part of the walk – finding the path down to that beach at Eyre. There is a lot of bracken growing in front of the ruin and the downhill route goes through this, parallel to the barbed wire fence, heading for another ruined building further down. It is difficult to see a clear path, particularly when the bracken is high between July and October, but there is only about 50 metres of it to wade through and you should be able to find the path again when you emerge on the other side. If not, just keep heading downhill towards that lower ruined building, bearing right through an obvious gap in a low bank and on down to cross a burn just before the ruin.

7. There are, in fact, two small ruined buildings and from here you have a choice of two paths; one of them goes straight ahead through a small copse and the other drops down to your right, going around the right side of these trees. Both arrive at crossing points over a fast flowing burn that comes down a small but steep gorge from your left. The ongoing route goes from the lower crossing point, which has a large flat rock at its edge, but this may be slightly more difficult to cross after heavy rain, so if you do cross over higher up then make your way back down the far bank, for about 50 metres, to the solitary rowan tree next to this lower crossing. You are now very close to the road but there is another short stretch of bracken to cross. From the rowan tree next to the burn crossing point, head through this high bracken for about 50 metres aiming for a small birch tree. You will then reach a grassy track that leads easily down to

a gate and onto the road below, perhaps some 2 hours after leaving the ferry.

8. Turn left and enjoy the ease of walking on a short section of tarmac that leads on to a grass and gravel track and then straight ahead through a gate and along a 'corridor' between two barbed wire fences. The small lighthouse at Eyre is on your right and to the left there is Stone Age burial capstone, a huge flat rock balanced on others, which is some 5000 years old and would originally have been covered by a large mound or cairn. Shortly after passing this there is a gap in the fence on your right and you can drop down to the beach to walk along the grassy edge of the shore heading northwards towards Fearns. You may have seals for company.

9. Just under a kilometre after passing the lighthouse you will come to the end of the fenced-off field on your left, and you can now move off the beach to walk along the grassy foreshore. You will see some of the houses of Fearns up on the hillside ahead of you as you make your way towards a wooded area.

Along the beach heading north towards Fearns (DS)

10. On reaching the wood, pick up a rather muddy path that heads through the hazel and birch trees just above the shoreline. This comes back towards the shore and then appears to end in the bracken but you can easily avoid this by heading back down to the beach. Just after passing some huts and boat houses at the edge of the beach you will have to cross a burn flowing into the sea. The water is quite shallow at the crossing point and should not be too difficult to ford in most weathers.

11. Once over the burn take the path, by the side of a large shed, and follow this uphill through the trees, bearing to your right below the white houses to reach the tarmac road behind the last of them. Now turn left onto the road and follow this for just over two miles to the junction near Inverarish. Turn left here if you want to visit the shop; otherwise continue straight on to follow your outgoing route back to the ferry terminal. On your way back you can enjoy views of the landscape sketched by Mairi Hedderwick. In her book *An Eye on the Hebrides* Mairi Hedderwick describes Raasay as a 'perfect rambling island. From strenuous to gentle the island provides a variety of walks, always with the hills of Skye dominating the western horizon.'

The old cart track route

There is a slightly shorter route between Eyre and Fearns following the 'Old Cart Track' which leaves the shoreline at the end of the fenced-off area mentioned in stage 9 above. This route is more difficult to follow and quite boggy in places but it starts at the corner of the fence and heads diagonally up to the line of birch trees edging the rising ground above the foreshore. Continue going uphill following a faint path near the edge of the escarpment on your right. Pass between two ruined buildings, across a boggy area and then ford a wide but shallow burn. There is a second burn to cross and when you reach a low bank, turn left to walk out of the trees and up onto the hillside. There are

End of the metalled rd.
N. Fearns -?
Raasay
Aug 24

traces of a path as you contour across the hillside, initially staying quite close to the line of the trees on your right but then beginning to move uphill heading towards the white house at Fearns. As you get closer to the road, aim for the post of a passing place slightly to the left of the white house and this will bring you to a crossing point over a burn which can be quite fast flowing after heavy rain. Once across, climb up the obvious path to the road and turn left to head back to the ferry.

Painting of the view from Fearns across the Suisnish Hill route towards Skye (MH)

With thanks to Mairi Hedderwick for permission to use the above image and quotations from An Eye on the Hebrides.

INVERARISH FOREST AND VIEWPOINT

A walk through the beech woods of Inverarish Forest before joining tracks through the coniferous forest with the option of climbing up to a cairned viewpoint overlooking the village.

START/ FINISH

Walk along the main road from the ferry, turning right at the low steading building (with clock tower) and bear left at the junction after the church. After approximately ½ kilometre take a left turn up the tarmac road and 300 metres later turn right into the Forestry Commission car park. The walk will finish back at the ferry terminal.

DISTANCE

6.5K/ 4½ miles

TIME

2 to 2 ½ hours

HIGHEST POINT

155 metres

GRADE/ ADVICE

Moderate to Difficult.
Mostly easy going on forest paths and tracks but there is a short section across trackless and rugged hillside so walking boots and a compass are advisable for this part. An alternative **Easier** route to the viewpoint, avoiding the worst of the rough ground, is given at the end of the main walk.

Route

1. Walk to the south end (to your right) of the Forestry Commission car park to follow a path up over a small hump, past a small stone building and then, just before reaching a broad track which enters the forest, take a narrower footpath to your right that runs along the edge of the pine trees and into a broadleaf woodland of mainly beech trees. As a short detour you may want to take one of the paths on your right that lead down into the middle of this fine beech wood. There is a route alongside the Inverarish Burn (described at the end of the main walk) but this can be very boggy at certain times of the year and you may be best to return to the higher and drier path.

2. The forest path slowly climbs above the burn and, after about 10 minutes from the car park, you will have a fine view to your right of waterfalls as the Inverarish Burn carves its way through the rocky gorge. When you come to the edge of the forest the path narrows, veering uphill to the left across an area of felled spruce, towards a ring of tall tree stumps which marks the site of an ancient stone circle. A few metres further on you will reach the start of a gravelled track but rather than following this, take a short cut on your left to cross about 50 metres of rough ground, choosing your footing carefully as there are hidden holes and tree branches in the long grass. Turn right to join the broad grassy track, referred to as the 'Burma Road', which was built by forest workers in the 1950s.

3. Walk along this grass roadway for about 450 metres, past one green Forestry Commission footpath marker post, until you see, on your right, a Raasay Paths Network (RPN) wooden marker post. Now look for a green Forestry Commission marker post on

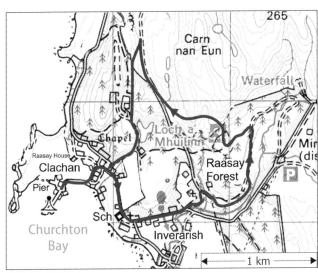

your left which marks the start of a gravel path that climbs sharply left and up to a clearing in the trees. Follow this track, muddy in places, and on through the forest up to a gate in the iron fence and out into a clearing.

Start of the walk through the Inverarish Forest (BH)

4. If you want to avoid all rough ground then continue along the track that takes you across the clearing and downhill into the forest again. This well-established path is quite steep and leads down, in about 5 or 10 minutes, to the tarmac road. Turn right and walk uphill for another 10 minutes to rejoin the route at stage 9 – see below.

5. If you are prepared for some rough and sometimes pathless terrain then turn right off the main path about 100 metres after the gate marked by a small cairn. Now follow a very faint path, bearing right and picking your way through the boggier parts, towards the bank of trees near the top right corner of this open area. Once you have reached the trees, walk diagonally uphill to your

Beech trees in the Inverarish
Forest (MF)

right until you come to the iron fence and the start
of a stone wall.

6. Climb steeply uphill, through the bracken and
heather, between the stone wall on your left and
the iron fence. The wall turns left but continue
on uphill, heading for an obvious gap on the crest
between two rocky mounds.

7. On reaching the crest make your way slightly
uphill across rock slabs to a deer fence that bars
the way to the summit of Carn nan Eun. Follow this
fence to your left (westwards) and downhill to a
gap in the wall. Follow the fence, over particularly
rough peaty ground, up to its corner on the crest of
the next ridge and then turn left to walk the short
distance down to the cairn. The effort is worth it

as the view over the village of Inverarish across to Skye as well as, to the left, the distant hills of Kintail is one of the best in the south of the island.

8. There is now an easier descent from the cairn to the road and you can just see the tarmac to the right of two telegraph poles with the prominent Skye hill of Ben Tianavaig in the background. This is the line to follow on an indistinct path through the grass and heather passing through a stand of small birch trees and down into a small boggy dip with a rhododendron bush. Continue downhill in the same direction towards the furthest telegraph pole, about 200 metres away, passing just to the right of this, and down to the tarmac road.

9. Turn right onto the road, across the cattle grid, passing a small cairn 100 metres on your left, and walk up to a picnic table which is a good place to stop and enjoy a view of the Trotternish hills on Skye. Now retrace your route back to that small cairn and follow a narrow rocky path, known by some as 'Cutting Edge', down the steep slope that zigzags to the right near the bottom and leads to a strange-looking wooden trestle-type stile across a

Looking over the south-west of Raasay towards Skye from the Viewpoint above Inverarish (TK)

fence. This structure was intended to form part of a see-saw crossing for intrepid mountain bikers but had to be abandoned and may now be rebuilt as a more traditional crossing point.

10. Once over the stile, walk along the path on your left through the trees, carpeted in moss, to reach the corner of a large wall that encloses the old orchard of Raasay House. Turn left along the wall to reach the gravelled tarmac road which goes downhill past Loch a' Mhuilinn and then bears right taking you down to the road at Clachan, just above the ferry terminal.

Alternative and easier route to the cairned viewpoint

If you want to avoid the worst of the rough ground on the main route you can still climb up to the viewpoint cairn directly from the road by reversing the route described in stage 8. The starting point is on the road just as it emerges from the forest near the picnic table. Head diagonally up the hill, on the right, initially on a fairly obvious path across the grass and heather slope, towards the telegraph pole. Keep going in a south-easterly direction, with the path disappearing occasionally, to pass the rhododendron bush in the dip and then the small stand of low birch trees. Head for the top of the ridge and you should reach the cairn in 15 to 20 minutes from leaving the road. Well worth it!

Alternative starting point for the walk

You can start the walk at the Forestry Commission information board just next to the stone built Henderson Bridge and find a path that runs along the side of the Inverarish Burn. This route is likely to be muddy in places and may prove impassable after very heavy rain. When you come to a large beech tree, keep to the right, where you'll see some stepping stones to help you cross a little stream that joins the main burn. Recent felling of spruce plantations has left what remains of the mature beech trees exposed and vulnerable; as a consequence many have fallen victim to recent gales. Still, there are signs of healing and regeneration; it is full of bird song on a good day and a lovely place to explore. Carry on past the massive railway pillars rising high above you, keeping the burn to your right. After several large fallen tree trunks the path narrows beside the burn through some rhododendron, to another clearing where bluebells put on a fine display in May. Carry on until you find the track beside the burn peters out just before a majestic larch tree, it's side branches each the size of a tree, pointing up to the sky. Follow the track to your left, diagonally uphill, until it joins the forest path described in section 1 of the main route.

This walk links up two former paths, the beech wood trail and a section of the path to Carn nan Eun, to make a circular route devised by the author.

FEARNS TO HALLAIG

The short walk along the track from Fearns to the Sorley MacLean memorial cairn is one of the best on the island and perfect for an afternoon wander. Continuing on to the deserted township of Hallaig is on rougher ground but the views of Raasay's east coast make it worth the effort.

Route

1. From the parking place at Fearns follow the grassy track heading north. It is generally dry underfoot in the summer months but sections in a wooded area can be boggy in winter. You can see faint lines across some of the flat areas to the right of the track where land was cultivated by the residents of the old township of North Leac. The crops were likely to have included potatoes, flax and barley.

2. The track remains fairly level for most of its way but gains some height as you near a finely constructed dry-stone walled area, thought to have been used as an animal enclosure. When the track turns the corner around the end of Beinn na Leac's high cliffs there is a grand view of Dun Caan and Raasay's rugged east coast.

START/ FINISH
The small parking place at the end of the public road to Fearns, just under 4 miles drive from the ferry.

DISTANCE
Memorial Cairn 5K/ 3 miles
Hallaig 9K/ 5½ miles

TIME
Memorial Cairn 1¼ hours
Hallaig 2½ hours

GRADE/ ADVICE
Easy. Short walk to the Memorial Cairn and back. **Moderate**. Continuing on to explore Hallaig involves crossing some rougher ground that may be muddy at certain time of the year.

The view of the east coast of Raasay from the Sorley MacLean memorial cairn (TK)

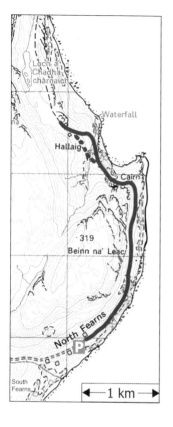

3. A few metres further is the memorial cairn erected 'In memory of the people of Hallaig and other cleared crafting townships' with the words of Sorley MacLean's poem 'Hallaig' inscribed in Gaelic and English on brass plaques. The poet was born at Oskaig on the west coast of Raasay in 1911 where Gaelic was the first language. His early poetry was in English but by the 1930s he became established as a writer in his native language. Hallaig is a meditative poem on the effects of the Highland Clearances, opening with the atmospheric line 'Time, the deer, is in the wood of Hallaig'.

4. The beach below you is a good place to hunt for fossils and get a closer look at the waterfall at the far end of the bay. If you want to visit Hallaig, continue along the track and enter the birch woods beneath the dark cliff passing a stone-built pony stable used by the estate for stalking parties. Keep contouring around the wooded slopes, taking care as the path is eroded in places and can be wet underfoot.

5. Follow the track out of the woods and head across the grassy hillside in the direction of Dun Caan. You should begin to see ahead of you the large stone-walled sheep fank at Hallaig as you begin to drop down towards the Hallaig Burn. The path begins to divide up with several ways across the burn but probably the most straightforward route is to stay close to the birch wood on your right and then follow the path through the trees and drop down to an obvious fording place.

6. Climb up the steep bank on the other side and the path will bring you out at the south-east

corner of the sheep fank, a structure that was built from the stones of the ruined houses after the land had been cleared. Now walk uphill along the outside of the wall to reach the south-west corner of the fank and an adjoining house ruin. You can follow a faint path up the grassy slope, in the direction of Dun Caan, to reach the other house ruins just in front of a great cleft in the rock, the Hallaig fissure.

7. Climb up the steep ridge to the south, away from the fissure, and walk to your left along the crest for a short distance to get a good view over the whole of the Hallaig township. It once housed 34 families with a total population of 127 but between 1841 and 1861 this number was reduced to 6. Many left on the emigration ships of 1852 and 1854, with others moving to the north of the island. Behind you, to the west, there are traces of former cultivation and paths that can be followed northwards to a nearby loch. For the return walk, retrace your steps heading towards the south-west

Hallaig Wood (RM)

Part of the ruined township near the Hallaig fissure (BH)

end of the sheep fank and following one of the paths to cross the Hallaig Burn.

8. There are fine views of the Cuillins on Skye as you near your starting point in Fearns. It was here that land was seized in 1921 by the men of Rona. They had repeatedly applied to the landowner and the Board of Agriculture for Scotland to be resettled in Fearns and Eyre to cultivate the more fertile parts of the island. These 'Raasay Raiders' were arrested and spent some weeks in prison before their claim was settled. You can still see the first house that they built on the road out of Fearns just before you come to the second of the more recently constructed white houses.

Additional information kindly provided Calum Don MacKay whose family have lived on Raasay and Rona for generations. His grandfather was one of the 'Raasay Raiders'.

Walking back to Fearns from Hallaig (RM)

BEINN NA LEAC LOOP

An exciting hill crossing to take a close look at the great fissure on Beinn na Leac before circling around the south of the hill and back to the starting point on the summit of the road to Fearns. There is also the option of walking along to the northern summit of Beinn na Leac to enjoy one of the finest views of Raasay's east coast.

Route

1. The starting point is the first passing place on the left as you start your descent from the summit of the road from Inverarish to Fearns. This is a large passing place so it should be easy to park and still leave room for its continued use by passing traffic. Head down the road towards Fearns for about 50 metres and then walk left, through the heather, to reach the bank of the Allt Fearns Burn.

2. The east (right) bank of the Allt Fearns burn offers the easiest way to start the climb up towards Beinn na Leac and is described in section 3 below. When the bracken is particularly high, in the summer months, it may be preferable to keep to the west

START/ FINISH
Near the summit of the road from Inverarish over to Fearns.

DISTANCE
Main loop: 3 K/ 2 miles
With summit: 6K/ 3½ miles

TIME
Main loop 1½ to 2 hours
With summit 2½ to 3 hours

GRADE/ ADVICE
Difficult. The main loop around the southern slopes of the hill is mainly on paths but the walk involves one river crossing and some sections of rough terrain.

The start of the route is considerably easier from October until June when the bracken has died back and the east (right) bank of the Allt Fearns burn can be followed. There is also a track along the edge of the west bank of the Allt Fearns but there is a trickier river crossing to negotiate and a steep bank to climb to join up with the east bank route.

The walk to the summit crosses mostly pathless terrain and care has to be taken to look out for any fissures which might be hidden by the heather.

The route is not suitable for young children or for dogs off the lead.

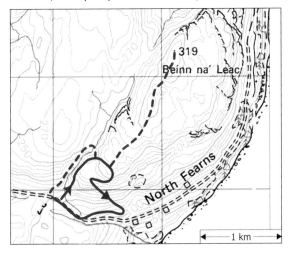

bank but there is significant erosion here and finding a way to cross the burn higher up is slightly more difficult. This alternative route is described in section 4.

3. Drop down the bank to find a way across the burn and then start to climb uphill, through the heather and bracken, following the river and heading towards a conical mound on the horizon. This shouldn't present any difficulty when the bracken has died back, and the route to the conical mound, though pathless, is fairly obvious. On reaching the top of the mound you will find a clear path to follow along the crest of the narrowing ridge, heading towards the large fissure which you can now see cutting through the slope of Beinn na Leac.

Looking up the Allt Fearns burn from the starting point on the road from Inverarish to Fearns (NF)

4. The alternative path to the west of the burn stays close to the lip of the Allt Fearns bank and follows this upstream to a boggy depression. Cross this and

The large rock fissure at the south end of Beinn na Leac (BH)

head for a gap in the rise ahead and either drop straight down to the river and cross, or continue along the sheep track to an obvious rock outcrop, a basalt dyke, where there is another opportunity to cross. If you don't like the look of either of these options, follow the sheep track over the top of the rock outcrop and make your way down to the burn for an easier crossing point. Once over the river climb diagonally up the steep bank, through the heather, heading in a general south-easterly direction. Make your way up to the top of the narrow ridge and turn left onto the path described for the east bank approach in section 3.

5. Drop down off the end of the short ridge, across a saddle and climb up the rocky path on the left side of the large rock fissure. Lying flat on the rocks at the top to look over the edge into the abyss is daunting enough for many of us but those dark green moss-covered rocks which you can see in the depths of the fissure are not even at the bottom of the cleft. They form a false base of chock stones with the fissure descending further into the hill, and it is possible to go through a gap in the end wall to climb deeper into the chasm. One of the rock climbs up the side of the fissure, close to where you may be lying, follows a large crack in the north face and is appropriately called 'Slow Release'. There is a distinct feeling that the side of this hill might be releasing rather quickly at some point in the future. There is a path that goes all the way around this fissure, passing above a prominent rock called 'The Leaping Stone' that juts out over the eastern end of the cleft. It got its name from some islanders who were photographed appearing to jump over to Scalpay as they leapt across the gap – and survived.

6. If you want to take the detour to the summit of Beinn na Leac head north-east and uphill to the top of the first rise before dropping down to cross a shallow valley and then up again to the next ridge. There are occasional sheep tracks but no distinct

The view from just north of the summit of Beinn na Leac (BH)

path to follow. You have to take care to avoid any small cracks or fissures in the heather, which is why it is not advisable to take dogs or small children with you. Make your way up and over another ridge, keeping to the highest ground, and on towards the small cairn on the top of the next rise. The summit of the hill is at the next cairn which you can see a few hundred metres away. The going is rough but the view from the summit cairn across to the cliffs of Dun Caan and the east coast of the island makes it all worthwhile. It is worth walking a short distance beyond the summit cairn to a very small lochan for an even better view – one of the finest on the island. There is a scrambling route from here down grassy gullies in the cliffs at the north-western end of the hill and on to Hallaig but our route recommends retracing your steps back to the large fissure at the south end of the hill. The complete detour along the summit ridge and back should not take much more than 50 minutes.

7. The 'Beinn na Leac Loop' route begins at the rocks at the eastern end of the main fissure and you start descending down the heather hillside in the direction of the northern tip of Scalpay, the neighbouring island to the south of Raasay. Just when you could be thinking that the ground is a bit steep you may spot some tyre marks on the track,

as this route is used by local mountain bikers. The path through the heather crosses a small natural bridge and just after this, turn to your right across another natural bridge and onto an obvious route through the heather. This contours round the side of the hill, keeping the same height, as it heads south-west and then due west to reach a gully.

8. Cross over the gully and climb up the other side to follow the path bearing left down the crest of the finely shaped ridge in the direction of Scalpay. The first of the white houses in Fearns comes in to view as you continue downhill, passing just to the right of an old metal fence.

9. Bear to your right to avoid some steep ground and make your way through the bracken to reach an established path coming in from your left. Walk up to your right, parallel to the road and the Allt Fearns burn that is carving its way through the soft grey-black glacial soil of the hillside, to join the road in about 10 minutes. A further 10 minutes brings you back to the passing place and your starting point.

Additional information on the design of this route was kindly provided by Steve White, a former mountain guide who lives on the island. He made the first ascent of 'Slow Release'.

View across to Scalpay from the start of the 'Beinn na Leac Loop' descent route (NF)

WALK TO INVER AND BAGH AN INBHIRE

START/ FINISH

Brae is five miles from the ferry terminal along the road to the north of the island, a few hundred metres after you pass the sign for Balmeanach. The signposted walk starts from a gate into the field on your left, just as the road climbs steeply out of a dip. There is room to park at the entrance but please leave your vehicle well clear of the metal gate to allow access for farm traffic.

DISTANCE

Main loop: 3K/ 2 miles

TIME

1½ to 2 hours

GRADE/ ADVICE

Easy. Sensible footwear advisable as the path is steep in places and often damp in the woods. A good walk at any time of year but particularly fine in August for the heather and in the autumn for the colour of the birch trees.

A beautiful walk through birch woods following the Inver Burn as it drops down to the sea. There are waterfalls and narrow gorges, and when the path leaves the woods it crosses heather clad slopes before arriving at a secluded beach, a favourite picnic spot for the Royal Family.

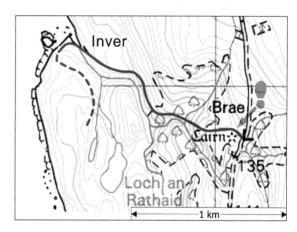

Route

1. Follow the signposted route to Inver (1.5K) through the gate, passing to the right of a ruined house, and enjoy a fine view across the Sound of Raasay to Portree on Skye as you head downhill through a field towards a metal gate.

2. Don't go through this gate but bear left to pick up a narrow but obvious path into the wood and, after a short distance, pass through a metal kissing gate with a Raasay Paths Network (RPN) sign.

3. The path drops steeply down through birch trees passing a rocky gorge on its way to the sea. There are waterfalls and canyons to look at, bridges to cross and ferns and lichens to see as you enjoy the magic of these woods. Some care is needed as the short

steep sections will be slippery when wet and the path
may seem particularly narrow as you look down from
on high into the deeper parts of the gorge.

Starting point for the walk to Inver (DC)

4. After about 25 minutes the path leads out of the
forest and on to the open hillside with the slopes
covered in heather – a fine sight in late August/
early September – with the views to the sea and
Skye opening up. You come to the first of the ruined
buildings of Inver, a township known to have existed
from the 16th century but abandoned by the end
of the 18th and since then only used as temporary
accommodation by fishermen and as holding areas
for sheep. After passing through another small
birch wood you arrive at the bay of Inver/ Bagh an
Inbhire, some 45 minutes from the road.

5. This is a good place to spend some time enjoying
the beach, sandy at low tide, exploring the cliffs and
the headlands or just looking at the views across
to Skye. There is also a cave on the right side of the
bay but the entrance is now partly hidden by two
holly trees. The Royal Family came ashore from the
Royal Yacht to visit the beach at Inver four times

Waterfalls on Inver Burn (DC)

in the 1970s and 80s, usually after a 'recce' by a group including one of the Royals. The Royal Yacht *Britannia* log records that it is 'a very good beach for picnics, BBQs etc as long as no midges... hill walking is good and sailing and water skiing can be done from the beach... but no room for games'. So you may have to carry a bit of equipment with you on your walk if you are going to make full use of the area.

6. It is worth finding a way across the burn to explore the whole of the bay – you may have to paddle or find some rather shaky stepping stones if you want to keep your feet dry. You can then have a closer look at the tidal headland at the southern end of the bay or cross the style over the fence at the back of the beach to explore the ruined buildings of the Inver township on your right. There are the remains of several buildings near the fence and a couple of houses on the ridge just up from the bay.

The path through the woods on the way down to Inver (DC)

7. Sea eagles can occasionally be spotted overhead or, with powerful binoculars, you may see them on

the other side of the Sound of Raasay swooping over the tourist boats that sail to the cliffs of Ben Tianavaig, just south of Portree – good eyesight or imagination needed.

8. It is possible to follow a faint path along the ridge heading south from the ruins of Inver to reach, in about 15 minutes, a high point, above a small lochan, and enjoy magnificent views in all directions. In fact, there is a route (largely pathless so a map and compass are advisable) from here continuing southwards along high ground and past another loch to the township of Balachuirn. But it is a long walk on the road back from there to your starting point.

9. The usual way back to Brae is to return uphill from the beach retracing your outward walk.

Additional information kindly provided by the staff of the Royal Yacht Britannia *at Ocean Terminal, Leith, Edinburgh.*

Inver Bay/ Bagh an Inbhire (DS)

A WALK TO DOIRE DOMHAIN

START/ FINISH

The main road to the north of the island, a kilometre north of the road sign at Glam/ Glame and some 5 miles from the ferry. After passing the farm buildings on your left at Glam drive on for a further kilometre until you reach a lay-by at the end of the fenced off area on your left (NG 562 437).

DISTANCE

4K/ 2½ miles

TIME

2½ to 3 hours

GRADE/ ADVICE

Moderate. There are some sheep tracks to follow but the route goes over rough ground which is muddy in places so walking boots recommended. A map and compass are useful but there are landmarks, streams and fences to help with navigation. Care is needed if you want to return along the coast as there are sheer cliffs, the tops of which are sometimes hidden by heather.

A walk down the Alt An Doire Dhomhain Burn to visit the deserted township of Doire Domhain and the ruined shieling where Prince Charles Edward Stuart is thought to have sheltered whilst hiding from the Redcoats.

Route

1. The buildings which you passed at Glam belong to the sheep farm and several times a year, during the 'gathering', sheep are brought here from the slopes of Dun Caan, Manish, Screapadal and other parts of north Raasay. The sheep know where they come from – they are 'hefted' – which means that when the gates of the farm pens at Glam are opened the sheep will make their way back to their own patch, turning right towards Dun Caan or heading north to their home in Manish. This is due to being bred for generations in the same area and they instinctively return to it for lambing. So if you get lost at least the sheep know where you are.

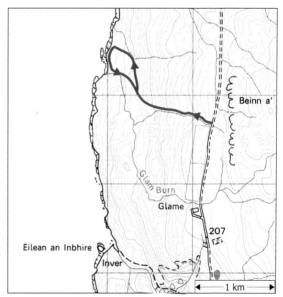

2. From the road, follow the fence line down rough grassy slopes, avoiding the worst of the boggy areas, heading towards the bay of Portree on Skye. After a couple of hundred metres, go left through the gate in the fence and walk down beside the Alt An Doire Dhomhain burn to reach a ruined stone building which is reputedly where Bonnie Prince Charlie sheltered for two nights in June 1746 whilst fleeing the Redcoats after the Battle of Culloden. There were soldiers searching for him on Skye and it was thought that he might be safer on Raasay. However, he felt uneasy here and returned to just north of Portree two days later before making his way to the Scottish mainland and back to France. The MacLeods did not lose their estate but the people of Raasay paid a heavy price for the laird's support of the rebellion with over 300 houses destroyed and almost all livestock killed.

The road at Glam near the start of the walk to Doire Domhain (CA)

3. Continue down the right/ north side of the burn following a raised bank and crossing a couple of

Stone ruin where Bonnie Prince
Charlie is reputed to have sheltered
whilst fleeing the Redcoats (NF)

side streams before dropping down a steep gully to
arrive at a flat grassy area with a large ruined house
and other smaller buildings, some 15 minutes after
leaving the road. Now go to your right to cross back
through a gate and follow the fence round to your
left.

4. The fence line turns sharply left after about
100 metres and passes around the back of a small
mound. After this you should see, to your right, a
narrow sheep track in the heather heading north
along the side of a series of low ridges. Follow this
path, heading in the direction of the small Holm
Island in the waters below the Storr mountain on
Skye, and you should just be able to see the stone
ruins of part of the deserted township of Doire
Domhain in the distance.

5. The sheep track becomes less obvious as you
cross grassy areas but the general direction should
be fairly easy to follow and you will soon come to
a large circular stone walled structure, close to a
small wood. A significant part of the Doire Domhain
township is just below the ridge and you can make

your way down steep slopes next to a burn or cross through the wood and follow a gentler slope down to the buildings. There are, in fact, settlements dating from the 16th to the 19th century spread across this whole area. The older buildings were possibly abandoned following the destruction caused by Government troops in 1746 but it was resettled in the 1820s and 1830s by islanders who had been cleared from other areas of Raasay. The population census for 1861/71 shows 3 families living in Doire Domhain.

6. There is a beautiful green area of cropped grass which leads down from the township ruins to the coast, and there are several tracks that you can follow as you head for a large square shaped rock at the shoreline, arriving no more than an hour after leaving the road. This is a good place for a picnic and the chance to explore the rocky shoreline. The most direct and safest return route is to retrace your outward journey heading back to the fence line alongside the Alt an Doire Dhomhain burn and up to the road. But the coastal scenery is so dramatic that you may prefer to return south along the shoreline, taking care as there are sheer drops which may be hidden by the heather.

7. There are sheep tracks for the first 200 metres along the top of the headland cliffs. Make sure that you follow them inland as they turn round the edge of the vertical cliffs which drop down to the bay where the Alt an Doire Dhomhain burn flows into the sea. Now walk alongside the ravine that runs inland from the bay until it turns sharply to the south and you can see, on your right, the burn cascading down in a series of waterfalls. Ignore the paths that follow the burn into the ravine, as it is a dead end for walkers, and, instead, climb up the gully straight ahead of you. Bear right when you reach the brow and head south-eastwards for some 400 metres, climbing slightly and following occasional traces of paths along the tops of low ridges.

Heading towards the ruined buildings of Doire Domhain with the Storr mountain on Skye (NF)

8. The lack of a continuous path makes this part of the route more difficult to follow but keep heading towards a stand of trees and you should see the line of fence posts which mark your return route. Turn left when you arrive at the fence and follow it around to the gate. Now head uphill along the bank of the burn, retracing your steps to arrive back at the road about half an hour after reaching the fence.

Additional information kindly provided by John 'Bradan' Gillies who farms at Glam.

MANISH MORE AND COASTAL WALK

A chance to explore the cliffs and rocks along this stunning stretch of coastline and visit the ruined township of Manish More.

Route

1. Walk northwards along the road to the next lay-by, halfway down the hill, and turn left onto the hint of a path. Cross some 50 metres over to a notch of piled stones and turn right to follow what looks like a low wall or grassed over bank of stones, heading north-west in the direction of The Storr mountain on Skye and the small Holm Island in the waters below it. This ancient wall is being slowly absorbed into the landscape so it may be difficult to see at times. There are only faint traces of tracks to follow

START/ FINISH

From a lay-by (NG 563 456) on the road to the north of the island, approximately 7½ miles from the ferry terminal. The road runs in a straight line after Glam/ Glame with one short twist down to the right before straightening again. Park at a lay-by on the left just before the road then drops down and makes a right angle turn eastwards. If you have made that sharp turn and are heading across the island then you have come too far!

DISTANCE

3½ K / 2 miles

TIME

2 hours plus

GRADE/ ADVICE

Moderate. The route crosses rough ground, only occasionally on clear paths, so walking boots recommended. A map and compass are advisable to ensure that you find your way back safely to the road.

The 'paths' along the coastline run very close to unfenced cliff edges at certain points so great care needs to be taken if walking with young children.

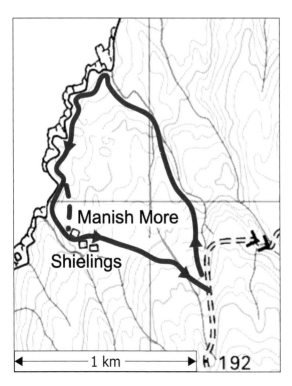

The inlet at the start of the coastal walk, south towards Manish More (NF)

but the best way down is fairly obvious if you keep to the higher ground on the ridge and aim for an inlet on the Raasay coast in line with Holm Island.

2. The ground is rough but you should arrive at the coast approximately 20 minutes after leaving the road and the view of those pink coastal rocks will make it all seem worthwhile. There is a pebbly bay with a large cave on the right of the inlet so plenty of places to explore before turning left to follow the coast southwards. The grain of this part of Raasay runs south-east/ north-west with the bedrock of Torridonian sandstone carved by dykes of igneous rocks creating a magnificent chaos of rock formations at the coast.

3. A few minutes after leaving the first inlet drop down to cross a flat boggy area and then climb up to join a sheep track. Some 5 minutes later the path divides with one strand going up to a rocky crest and the other heading towards the coast. If you follow the latter you will understand why some sheep preferred the other option as, in a few metres, you find yourself standing on the edge of cliffs that circle the bay. This cove is large enough to have its own tidal island in the centre. If you enjoy scrambling then you will no doubt make your way down to the bottom of the cliffs to explore the rock formations. But the other route offers an easier option and will take you round the edge of the bay to continue along the coast.

4. The sheep obviously enjoy this coastal walk because there are plenty of tracks to follow but watch out for the occasional collapsed hole in the ground. About 10 minutes later you will come to the cliffs which guard the next bay and you can make your way around the edge to reach a grass and rock ramp that drops down and allows you to explore the grand rock arch that leads, at low tide,

to another secret bay.

5. At the side of the rock arch a track continues southwards climbing up the slope and then turning right to continue along the coast. The next bay is hidden from view and you have to start heading slightly inland and

Rock arch on the coastal walk (NF)

climb up to a rocky knoll to avoid steep cliffs ahead. Cross the top of the burn which runs into the bay and either start to scramble down a rocky path towards the beach or make your way around the top of the bay. The latter option traverses round the top of the cliffs and onto a ridge which will take you direct to the ruined township of Manish More but you will miss seeing some dramatic seascapes in an area which is a haven, in the spring, for nesting birds such as fulmars and kittiwakes.

6. The relatively easy scrambling route descends down to the gully and across to a narrow and

Cliffs near Manish More (NF)

somewhat eroded path which climbs up through the heather. It is then a level walk through bracken and heather, keeping close to the coast but take great care because some tracks go very near to the cliffs and the edge is sometimes hidden by heather. Soon you will be able to look across at the cliffs which line the great coastal ravine that leads

inland to Manish More – views which may tempt you ever nearer to the edge. But a combination of bracken and heather underfoot is designed to trip photographers walking backwards to get that perfect shot. All paths now travel in the same direction, heading inland passing waterfalls on the Manish More Burn to reach the township.

7. The tree-lined gully provides shelter for several houses, all of them with rounded corners. This, I am reliably informed, dates them as being built before 1840 because thereafter houses were constructed with right-angled corners and gable ends. The rounded corners made it easier to thatch the roof so it was nothing to do with stopping evil spirits from hiding in the corners. In 1841 there were 40 people living in Manish. Ten years later this population had halved and by 1861 the area was emptied to make way for sheep.

Rock formations on the shoreline near Manish More (RM)

8. To return to the road lay-by, no more than 20 minutes from Manish More, head inland, initially following a path just to the north of the buildings, and then aim for the highest point directly due east. The path disappears but it is relatively easygoing making your way through the heather and up to the high ground. The lay-by should now come into view as you continue eastwards across undulating ground to reach the road. This return route could be used for a very short outing to Manish More, perhaps out and back in less than an hour.

Additional information kindly provided by island resident Margaret Moodie.

MANISH BEG AND MANISH POINT

START/ FINISH

This walk starts on the main road to the north of the island some 8 miles from the ferry terminal. After travelling over 7½ miles up the western side of Raasay the road turns sharply to the right to head east across the island before dropping steeply downhill to another sharp bend. Park in the first lay-by on the left after this bend (NG 567 458), leaving enough space for other traffic to use the passing place.

DISTANCE

6.5K / 4 miles

TIME

4 to 5 hours (to allow time for exploring the coastal area)

GRADE/ ADVICE

Moderate to Difficult. This is a wild coastal area and use of a map and compass can help you check that paths, which you will come across from time to time, are taking you in the right direction. The ground is boggy in places so walking boots advisable.

A walk to the ruined township of Manish Beg and along the dramatic coastal scenery of the area around Manish Point. There are remote beaches, cliffs and caves to explore before heading back through a green wilderness, passing three beautiful lochans to reach the road about ¾ mile north of your starting point.

Route

1. Head due north from the lay-by, initially across a flat boggy area, heading towards a low flattened mound on slightly higher ground. There are traces of a path and in just over 10 minutes you reach a flattish mound, which is the start of a long ridge running northwards. You can follow the crest of this ridge until you see, in the distance, the stone ruins of Manish Beg down in the glen on your right. The driest and most scenic route is to stay on this ridge all the way down to a heather spur just west of the township, arriving at the ruined houses about half an hour after leaving the road.

2. The deserted hamlet with its dozen or so former buildings is in a beautiful setting with views out to the Sound of Raasay and across to Skye. Together with Manish More this area of Raasay housed a total of 40 people in 1841 but 20 years later it was cleared.

3. Walk along a path between the houses then head north and downhill to the west bank of the Manishbeg Burn which is coming down from your right. Keep following this burn for the half mile down to the bay on the coast. Some of the ground is rough going but there are traces of tracks and some high ground to follow to avoid the boggiest parts. You will cross the burn, just before it reaches

the bay, and arrive at the shore with its mound of rounded stones on the beach.

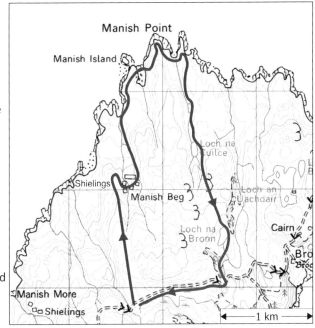

4. There is a stone wall on the right side of the bay and a path next to this which you can take to climb up onto the headland. From here there are several animal tracks to follow northwards along the coast to the next inlet where there is a tidal lagoon on the landward side of the beach. To continue to Manish Point walk across the large rocks between the shoreline and the lagoon, and find a narrow path through bracken which climbs steeply up the low cliffs on the eastern side of the inlet. Near the top of the cliffs you can look

Ruined buildings of the Manish Beg township (NF)

The coastline near Manish Point
looking north towards Loch Arnish (DS)

back to see Manish Island and, from the top of the headland, enjoy the fine views across Loch Arnish to Torran.

5. Keep your height for the next 100 metres or so before dropping down to your left to take a look at Manish Point. Take care because there is a deep fissure, like a rock crevasse, that fractures this part of the north coastline so look for a rock bridge to get to the end of Manish Point. It looks as if this northern tip of the coast has almost been snapped off with a clean cut right through the neighbouring headland to the east. There are rocks to scramble over and caves to visit, so you may be tempted to follow paths eastwards for a longer exploration of this dramatic coastline.

6. The most direct route back to the road starts from the end of the 'severed' unnamed headland just east of Manish Point and heads inland to the south, keeping on high ground, just to the left (east) of the burn which links two lochans with the sea. These are particularly beautiful on a sunny

summer's day when the water lilies are in full bloom. (There is also an alternative path on the other ridge to the west of the burn.)

A rock fissure on the headlands near Manish Point (RM)

7. You have to drop down to cross some wet ground to walk around the reeds at the eastern edge of the second lochan, Loch na Cuilce, before following a faint path which climbs up the ridge aiming for the left of a rocky knoll on the skyline. The crest of the ridge just beyond this knoll is a great place to

The last of the three lochans, Loch na Bronn (NF)

stop to enjoy the views across Loch Arnish towards Eilean Fladday and eastwards over to Applecross and the cliffs at Screapadal. You may also welcome the sight of the road in the distance but a third lochan, Loch na Bronn, is hidden from view. In fact, it is close by and you soon see it as you begin to drop downhill to walk around its eastern edge on a clear path through the grass and heather before heading up and along the top of a low ridge towards a copse of trees.

8. Walk through the birch trees and along to the end of the ridge. Follow the clear path (animal track) that drops down and then up again through the heather aiming for a pole marking a passing place on the road, a short distance away. Turn right onto the tarmac and it is only about a 15 minute walk back to your starting point.

Additional information kindly provided by Liz and Robin Millar who are both keen walkers and have a house on the island. Liz's father was born in Kyle Rona in 1916 and moved to Brochel in 1923.

SCREAPADAL AND BROCHEL CASTLE

A chance to escape any westerly wind and visit the deserted townships of North and South Screapadal which nestle under the high cliffs of the east coast. There are fine views over the Inner Sound to Applecross, and the chance to explore a beach as well as visiting nearby Brochel Castle.

Route

1. Walk down the track from the parking area and go through the metal gate which marks the entrance into the, now felled, Screapadal forest. Follow this broad track as it zigzags down to the coast, with the views of Raasay's east coast cliffs and over the Inner Sound to Applecross opening up before you. Keep an eye out for seals in the water and you might be lucky and spot an eagle flying overhead.

2. As the track turns sharply to the right just before flattening out there is a small path coming in from

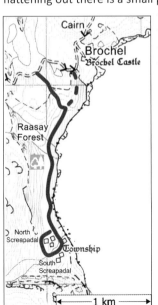

the left which can be taken to Brochel if you want to walk to the castle as part of your return route.

3. Continue along the main track crossing two burns, the second on a substantial footbridge over a gorge. The route now follows a narrower path staying at the same height above the shoreline, heading southwards towards the prominence of

START/ FINISH
Follow the road to the north of the island for about 8½ miles from the ferry. Half a mile before reaching Brochel Castle you should see a lochan across to the left and then come to a parking area opposite, on your right, a group of small birch trees and a track leading down to a metal field gate.

DISTANCE
5K/ 3 miles

TIME
2 hours (allow more if visiting Brochel Castle)

GRADE/ ADVICE
Easy. A walk along tracks and paths and a good choice if the wind and rain are coming from the west. The climb to the top of the townships on the steep grassy hillside and the crossing of the burn, An Leth-allt, are slightly more demanding but it is not necessary to include this part of the route to enjoy the walk. The diversion along the path to Brochel is on slightly rougher ground.

A view down the east coast of Raasay from near the start of the walk to Screapadal (DC)

Candle Rock, part of the cliffs which form the dramatic backdrop to Screapadal, the 'dale of the moving scree'.

4. About 30 minutes after leaving the road you should arrive at a small metal gate in the stone wall that marks the end of the forest and the beginning of the deserted township of North Screapadal. You can remain on the main path which crosses a ford before arriving a short distance later at South Screapadal but, if possible, climb up the grassy hillside to fully appreciate the layout of the former dwellings of the northern township.

5. It is a steep slope but the views just get better as you climb past the ruined buildings and up to a large solitary rock above the last house. The north and south townships are separated by the An Leth-allt burn and you can make your way across the hillside to find a suitable crossing point. The sides of the burn are quite steep at this point and you

may prefer to climb slightly higher, to just above the trees on the river bank, to find an easier place to cross. You can now walk down the south side of the burn to reach the houses of South Screapadal or explore the base of the cliffs that tower over the townships and the cave which was reputedly used for the illicit distilling of whisky.

6. South Screapadal is smaller than its northern neighbour but very atmospheric. It may be difficult to appreciate that there were some 26 families, about a hundred people, living in these townships as recorded in the 1841 census. Ten years later this had almost halved and by 1861 the buildings were empty and the area cleared for sheep farming.

7. You can drop down the grassy hillside from South Screapadal to reach the main path near a heavily fortified shed. This construction, along with the nearby tall marker posts, is linked to Royal Navy submarine testing which is carried out in the Inner Sound. In his powerful poem 'Screapadal', Sorley MacLean makes a link between a nuclear submarine lifting 'its turret and its black sleek back' with its capability to 'leave Screapadal without beauty just as it was left without people'.

The walk along the grassy track along the coast towards Screapadal (RM)

8. Turn left onto the path and drop down to ford the burn before reaching the metal gate and returning along the path and track towards your starting point. If you have time, it is worth visiting the beach where there is a good picnic spot at the south end. You should find an easy way down about 300 metres after crossing the second of the two footbridges.

9. If you want to walk to Brochel Castle, take the

Looking south towards
Candle Rock from the ruins of
Screapadal (RM)

footpath mentioned on the outward route that
goes off to the right just as the main track starts
to climb up the hillside. The narrow path weaves
its way for about 600 metres through felled forest,
with fine views over the coastline, to reach a metal
gate at the road down to Brochel. There is a path
to the beach near the large parking area and, after
looking at the castle, it is a short half mile walk back
up the road to the start of your route.

The castle was built in the 15th century and
was the seat of the first of the MacLeod chiefs
of Raasay, Calum Garbh, son of the 9th Chief of
Lewis. It overlooks the main sea route from Kyle of
Lochalsh to Lewis and raiding of passing ships was
a profitable business. Whether this was carried out
by 'clanless, broken men' who had sought refuge
on Raasay during this period or organised by the
MacLeods themselves is still debated. The last of
the MacLeods to live in the castle was Chief Iain
Garbh who is thought to have died in 1671, and the
clan chiefs then moved to Clachan in the south of
the island. The castle is built on agglomerate stone
and, despite this relatively unstable foundation, it

was designed to have three floors and was certainly still in relatively good condition when James Boswell visited it in 1773 – 'it does not appear to have mouldered'. It is still a very impressive sight today but there are definite signs of 'mouldering'.

Additional information and checking of this route kindly provided by island residents Jill and David Westgarth.

Brochel Castle (yR)

CALUM'S ROAD AND NORTH ARNISH

START/ FINISH

Allow plenty of time to drive the 9 long miles from the ferry to Brochel. There are parking spaces on the left at the end of Calum's Road.

DISTANCE
4.5K/ 3 miles

TIME
2 to 2½ hours

GRADE/ ADVICE

Easy. An easy walk to the township of North Arnish. **Moderate**. The ongoing coastal/ hill walk has been classed moderate as because, whilst there are intermittent tracks to follow, they disappear near the summit viewpoint and you have to find your way down steep slopes on the return. It is boggy in places so boots are advisable.

This route begins with an exhilarating 1¾ mile drive from Brochel Castle along Calum's Road to Arnish. The circular walk visits the old township of North Arnish then follows a route high above the east coast, with fine views over to Applecross and Torridon, and up to a cairned viewpoint.

Route

1. The road from Brochel to Arnish is not just a scenic marvel, 'a landscape sculpture' to quote from Roger Hutchinson's excellent book *Calum's Road*, but also a striking example of one man's heroic effort to save a community. There is a cairn at the roadside, shortly after leaving Brochel, to commemorate the work of Calum MacLeod who, almost single-handedly, built, with just a pick-axe and wheelbarrow, a road from his home in Arnish to the public road end at Brochel – in the hope that 'new generations of people would return to the north end of Raasay'.

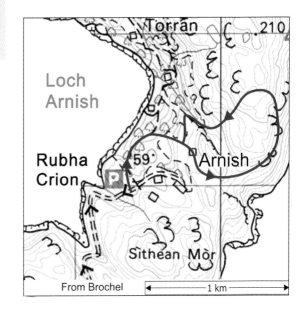

2. From the cairn 'the reckless panorama of eastern Raasay unfolds' (Roger Hutchinson, 2006). Loch an Uachdair, hidden from view, is on your left shortly after leaving the cairn and otters can occasionally be seen heading seawards along the loch burn.

The start of Calum's Road in the north of the island (DS)

3. From the car park at Arnish walk up to your left to the 'End of Public Road' sign and follow the rough vehicle track, signposted to Torran (900m), downhill on your left. Cross through the gate/ stile and 100 metres later turn right off the main track up a grassy bank which heads up towards a gap in the birch wood.

4. Turn left when you emerge from the trees to walk uphill on a grassy path through the bracken to reach the ruined buildings of the former township of North Arnish.

5. The long building with the gable ends was for housing and a former post office for the north of the island. Two families would have lived here, one at either end with the post office in the central section. The census for 1861 records that there were 7 families, totalling 45 people, living in Arnish.

Aerial view of part of Calum's Road (GR)

6. To continue on to the viewpoint, walk up behind the former post office, bearing slightly right to climb up onto a ridge. Follow the path along its crest, above some more ruined buildings, before dropping down left to cross over to the parallel, more northerly ridge, traversing eastwards. The coast soon comes into view and then the path, not much more than an animal track, bears round to the north and drops down steeply to near the corner of a fence. It is a low sheep fence, easy enough to cross without causing any damage, and you should be able to see the path heading onwards as it contours, high above the shoreline, around the craggy hillside. This hill is named on the OS map as Meall Dearg Arnish but is known locally by another name.

7. There are very fine views up and down the east coast of Raasay and over to Applecross. A short time later, as you steadily climb along the hillside,

the hills of Torridon come in to view. There are rock pavements of pink gneiss to cross interspersed with sections of boggy grassland and the path becomes less obvious. Avoid losing height and continue to contour round the hill until you reach a large coastal cleft or inlet which will force you to bear left, away from the coast, and uphill. You should pass a very small lochan, little more than a large puddle, about 30 minutes after leaving North Arnish.

8. There is no obvious path at this stage but continue making your way uphill and head for a cairn on the near horizon, which you should reach about 10 or 15 minutes from the lochan. There are views across to the west coast and up to the north of Raasay and on a nearby summit, just to the west, you should see a large balanced boulder and what looks like a white drum. It is a relay station allowing internet access for the north of the island and Applecross.

9. Walk across to this summit to begin the return route that heads south-west towards, in the distance, a white house with, currently, a green corrugated roof. You may spot a black cable running along the ground from the relay signal equipment and it goes all the way back to Arnish, much of the time on your route, so take care to avoid damaging this power supply. There are steep cliffs immediately below the summit, so bear to your left to traverse eastwards through the crags of pink gneiss, passing an impressive rock face at the bottom which has a shelter beneath it. Cross the low sheep fence at the corner/ straining post near a stone built sheep fank and pick up a rather indistinct path over the next rise, heading for a stand of birch trees on the main ridge ahead.

10. Cross a gap through a low stone wall in the next dip where you will see another sheep fank on your right. The path becomes more obvious as you climb up. Follow the line of trees along the edge of the

View over to Loch Arnish from
North Arnish (NF)

hillside heading first westwards, and then to the
south, around the end of the ridge, and back to
reach the former post office building.

11. Now retrace your outgoing route along the
grassy track between the buildings and the bracken,
heading downhill towards Loch Arnish. Turn right
when you reach the small birch trees and follow the
grassy path down through the trees to the Torran
track where you turn left to head back for South
Arnish.

*Additional information kindly provided by Julia MacLeod,
daughter of Calum MacLeod.*

EILEAN FLADDAY/ FLADDA

From the road end at Arnish there is a fine walk past the township of Torran and along a path through the heather, high above the coast, before dropping down to a causeway and across to the tidal island of Fladday.

START/ FINISH
Allow plenty of time to drive the 11 long miles from the ferry to Arnish. There are parking spaces on the left at the end of Calum's Road.

DISTANCE
6K/ 4 miles

TIME
2 to 3 hours

GRADE/ ADVICE
Easy. If you are planning to go to the island then sensible footwear needed to cross over the rocks and/ or seaweed at the causeway. Check tide times for Portree (www.tidetimes.org.uk) and allow yourself no more than 3 hours either side of low tide to explore the island – two might be safer.

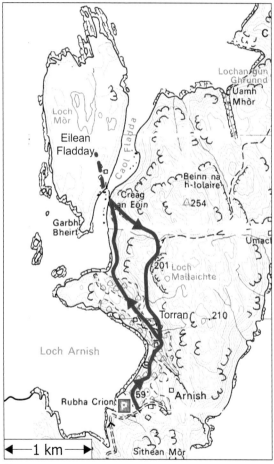

Route

1. From Arnish follow the rough vehicle track signposted to Torran (900m) and Kyle Fladda (2.8K) downhill and, after crossing a stile, enter the newly

Looking across Loch Arnish
towards Torran (DS)

established woodland area. Continue straight ahead at the path junction behind the first house in Torran taking the Raasay Paths Network (RPN) sign for Fladda. This house, now a holiday home, used to be the old school house and the children from Fladday walked this route every school day until the teacher for a 'side' school was established on the island. If the tides were against them they missed school or didn't get home in the afternoon. At least two applications to the council to build a short footbridge were rejected.

2. The track now goes through some trees and towards a dip in the hills before emerging onto the hillside with the rocky shoreline far below you. This is a good walk at any month of the year but probably the best time is late August/ early September when the ling heather is in full bloom and the scent stirred by your footfall. This fine path that weaves its way in and out of the heather was also built by Calum MacLeod, this time with his brother's help.

3. A little way along you will see, to your left, a very short path to a large flat rock where you can get your first sight of the three white houses on Fladday, some 20 minutes' walk away. Tall heather may conceal some short sections but generally the path is easy to follow. After going through a wooden swing gate the route heads inland and up to the crest of the ridge from where you can look down on the dark green waters of the bay leading

to the causeway across to the island. There may
be herons on patrol and, if you are lucky, an otter
searching the shoreline.

4. About halfway down to the bay you will pass an
RPN sign on your right that marks the start of the
path to Caol/ Kyle Rona which will be followed for a
short time on the return route. There are steps for
the steepest sections down to the causeway and
then you have to decide whether you prefer to cross
rocks and seaweed to reach the sandy causeway
or follow one of the narrow paths which scramble
a few feet uphill and round to a drier part of the
crossing. These latter paths are on steep ground and
badly eroded so they are not the best option if you
don't enjoy clinging to rocks and heather to keep
your balance.

5. Once across the causeway head for a metal gate
just to the right of the shed and follow the path
uphill onto the headland. Behind the second white
house there is a grassy path which leads up to the

The path towards Eilean Fladday/ Fladda (NF)

top of a cairned mound, named
from the Gaelic as 'sight hill', and
there is a fine view across the island
with Loch Mor in the distance.
The walk up to this point will have
taken about an hour from Arnish.
The absence of sheep and cattle
these days means that the island
paths have been overgrown, and
so further exploration of Fladday is
difficult but you may want to try and
make your way down to the shores
of one of the lochs or across to the
west coast. The '-ay' at the end of
the name Fladday is Old Norse for
'island' and it may well have been
occupied by the Vikings. Some
burnt pine trees were found by the
islanders when cutting peat and the
trunks were buried some 30 feet

deep in the ground. This indicates that the fire might have taken place as long ago as the era of Norse occupation when the fabled daughter of the Norse king reputedly burnt them down in spite.

The isle of Fladda/ Eilean Fladday (RM)

6. There were up to 7 houses occupied in Fladday in the late 19th century with a population of over 50. The last permanent residents who lived in the three white houses that you see today, now holiday homes, left in 1965. The remaining buildings include a house which was thatched – remembered as being the warmest of them all – and several outhouses for animals and the storage of potatoes, grain, hay and peat. The families worked the land together, each usually owning a couple of cows, some sheep and hens. Most supplies were brought in by boat from Portree and harvesting the sea was an important part of their lives. You may be able to see a stone-walled fish trap or pen down on the shore near the causeway which, after a good tide, could be brimming with a catch of small fish, mostly saithe, which would be salted and stored for cattle feed.

7. After crossing the causeway on the return journey and climbing up the steps, take the path to your left, marked by an RPN sign, which heads inland and uphill through the heather. There is a short section overgrown, in summer months, by bracken but the path becomes clear when you reach the crest of the rise and easy to follow, eastwards, to reach, in about 20 minutes, a major junction of paths marked by another RPN signpost.

The route to the left goes to Kyle Rona with options of climbing the nearby summit of Beinn na h-Iolaire, but the route for this walk turns right to follow the signpost back to Torran.

8. The ground is boggy on your right as the path goes beneath the cliffs of Meall Dearg but the terrain improves after a few minutes once you reach a stile and gate. Crossing rock slabs between mounds you begin to go downhill and the view opens up to reveal a magnificent panorama across Loch Arnish to the cliffs of Dun Caan and the Skye hills beyond. There is more heather lining the path before it descends into the birch woods, and approximately 20 minutes after the Fladday/ Kyle Rona path junction you will arrive at Torran where you turn left on the main track back to Arnish.

Additional information kindly provided by Calum Gillies who was born and brought up on Fladday and his wife, Catriona, who joined him on the island when she was appointed teacher at the school.

Heading south on the way back
towards Loch Arnish (RM)

BEINN NA H-IOLAIRE AND UMACHAN

START/ FINISH

There are parking spaces on the left at the end of Calum's Road at Arnish which is 11 long miles from the ferry so allow plenty of time to drive there.

DISTANCE

Beinn na h-Iolaire: 7K/ 4.5 miles

Including Umachan: 10K/ 6 miles

TIME

Beinn na h-Iolaire: 2 to 3 hours

Including Umachan: 4 to 5 hours

HIGHEST POINT

233 metres

GRADE/ ADVICE

Moderate. The ascent of Beinn na h-Iolaire is mostly on clearly signed paths. Only the short final ascent is over open ground although there are a few cairns marking the route.

The route to Umachan is **Difficult.** The path is faint at the start but becomes clearer after a couple of hundred metres. There is, however, a tricky descent on a steep traverse down to the bottom of a gully to reach the township.

Beinn na h-Iolaire, the hill of the eagle, is the highest point in the north of the island and provides magnificent views over this part of Raasay and across to the islands of Rona, Eilean Tigh and Fladda. The relatively easy climb, after the walk in from Arnish, starts near a major junction of paths and its ascent can easily be combined with visits to Kyle Rona, Eilean Fladday or the township of Umachan (included as part of this walk).

Route

1. Follow signs to Kyle Rona from the parking place at Arnish and walk down the rough vehicle track northwards to Torran. After crossing the stile into the newly established woodland area, continue on the track and when you come to the first house in Torran follow the sign to Rona on the right, uphill through a wood of birch, hazel and some rowan.

2. The path emerges from the wood after about 10 minutes of ascent giving great views across to the Trotternish hills and back to the Cuillins on Skye. A few minutes later you reach a stile and gate and if you walk a few metres to the left of this you

The path to Torran (TK)

should see the white OS pillar in the distance at the top of the hill straight ahead of you. This is Beinn na h-Iolaire.

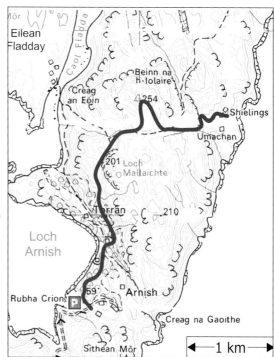

3. The land flattens out as the path goes between the cliffs of Meall Dearg on your right and a boggy area to your left, and you may catch another glimpse of that OS pillar. Go straight ahead at the next path junction, where the route from Fladda joins, and about 2 minutes later you will see a large cairn on your left just as the path turns to the right. Keep on the path as it climbs a steep rise, and then when it flattens out (and before it starts to climb again) head up the hill to your left, passing a small pile of stones some 20 metres from the path, that almost resembles a cairn. Keep heading towards the highest point on the horizon as you climb up over large plates of ice scraped Lewisian gneiss rock to reach the summit some 1¼ hours after leaving Arnish. There is a small lochan at the top as well as that gleaming white OS pillar and a panoramic view across the top of the island, over to Torridon and Applecross, down the cliffs of Raasay's east coast and across to Skye. A short walk over the rock slabs to the eastern end of the summit gives you a view down to Eilean Fladday. And, just in case you are interested, this is a 'Marilyn' – one of Scotland's 1200 hills that have a drop of at least 150 metres on all sides.

4. Retrace your steps if you are returning direct to Arnish. If continuing to Umachan, follow the summit ridge just slightly to the east, to avoid some peat hags, and then due south to reach the main path at

View looking northwards from the
summit of Beinn na h-Iolaire (RM)

an obvious bealach, marked by a large cairn on top
of a mound on the far side. Turn left onto the path
heading towards the east coast.

5. After about 400 metres you will see, on your right,
a wooden Raasay Paths Network (RPN) post marking
the start of the path to Umachan. There is little more
than an imagined path to begin with as you leave
the Kyle Rona route to drop down the gully heading
towards the east coast but one starts to emerge
as you walk through the heather. (When is a path
a path? When someone ahead of you says it is?)
Keep following the burn on your right, crossing a gap
through a low stone wall or bank, staying on higher
ground wherever possible.

6. Some 400 metres after leaving the main path at
the marker post you will arrive at the top of a steep
rise or cliff and you can now look down towards
the sea, although Umachan is still hidden behind a

further ridge. It looks, at first, as if there is no easy way down as there is steep ground to your left and waterfalls and a rock band on the right. However, it is possible to traverse down to your left, starting with following the path some 20 metres to the right and then turning left near to the edge and downhill on small rock ledges which are steep but not exposed. Continue to traverse round the hillside climbing up slightly to avoid bracken and some small pools of water until you can easily drop down to the bottom of the gully passing round the back of a large tree and crossing over the burn which runs underground at this point.

7. The path now bears to your right and over the next ridge to reveal the ruined buildings of Umachan below you, approximately 25 minutes after leaving the main path. Census figures show a population of 22 people (4 families) lived here in 1841 but with the clearing of people in the south of Raasay this doubled to 43 (8 families) by 1861. It was poor land and one of the hardest places on Raasay to make a living. As a relative of one of the former residents said, 'A week in Umachan was considered too long' – and some lived there for over 40 years. The best preserved house with well constructed stone walls, still with a gable end, chimney and fireplace, is across to your left, just north of the other buildings. This house once belonged to the grandmother of the lead singer of the punk rock band, The Clash. Joe Strummer had always wanted to visit this family home but he died before he had the chance to do so. Two other members of the group, however, did come across to Raasay and left hidden some items in memory of Joe. Local resident, Paul Camilli, gives more information about this in his entertaining 'Life at the end of the road' blog for 5th September 2010, where he records his visit by boat to Umachan.

8. A more direct return to the Kyle Rona path could be made from the bottom of the gully and climbing up the hillside over rough ground heading due west.

The deserted township of
Umachan (DS)

However, there is not even a hint of a path and
our route recommends retracing your steps on the
return journey, up to the top marker post and over
the bealach to arrive back in Arnish approximately
1½ hours after leaving Umachan.

*Additional information kindly provided by Paul Camilli
who lives in Arnish and is the author of a great blog 'Life
at the end of the Road' which has lots of photographs and
information about life on Raasay.*

CAOL/ KYLE RONA AND EILEAN TIGH

A beautiful walk from Arnish to the remote north of Raasay giving open views across this wild coastal landscape of Lewisian Gneiss, some of the oldest rocks in the world. You may want to cross over to the tidal island of Eilean Tigh for a panoramic view of the Raasay archipelago.

START/ FINISH
There is parking on the left at the end of Calum's Road at Arnish which is 11 long miles from the ferry so allow plenty of time to drive there.

DISTANCE
13K/ 8 miles return to Kyle Rona

TIME
5 to 6 hours return walk from Arnish to Kyle Rona

6 to 7 hours if including Eilean Tigh

GRADE/ ADVICE
Difficult. This is a long walk in wild and isolated country and some sections will be boggy. A path can be followed for nearly all of the route but taking a map and compass with you is advisable. Check tide times (www.tide times.org.uk for Loch A'Bhraige area) if intending to cross over to Eilean Tigh and allow yourself a maximum of 2 hours either side of low tide to explore the island.

Walking up through the woods from Torran (RM)

Route

1. This route is signposted from the parking place at Arnish – 4 miles to Kyle Rona according to a metal sign but 8 kilometres on the wooden footpaths sign! Follow the rough vehicle track northwards to Torran, over the stile and into the newly established

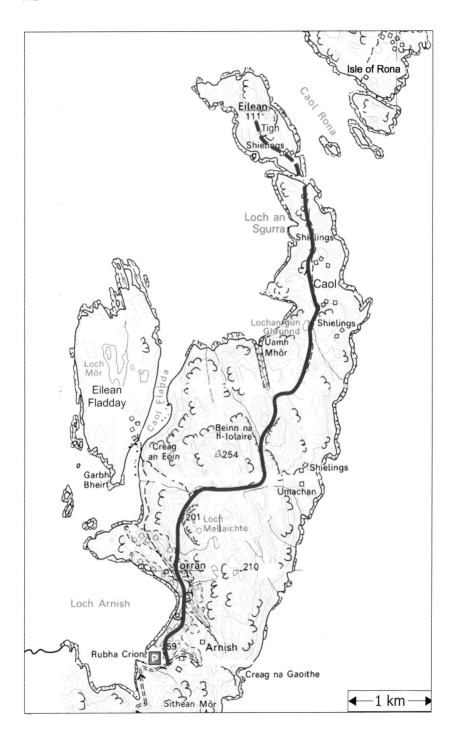

Following the path to Caol/ Kyle Rona (RM)

woodland area. At the back of the first house in Torran follow the sign to the right, uphill through a wood of birch, rowan and hazel.

2. The path emerges from the wood after about 10 minutes of ascent giving great views across to the Trotternish hills and the Cuillins on Skye. A few minutes later you reach a stile and gate as the land flattens out between the cliffs of Meall Dearg on your right and a boggy area to your left.

3. Go straight ahead at the next path junction, where the path to Fladda joins on your left, and head uphill for a 15 minute climb to the bealach. The path turns east and you begin to see over to Applecross and the Torridon hills in the distance. Pass another footpath sign before bearing northwards around the slopes of Beinn na h-Iolaire to reach the Bealach Chruidh.

4. There is a short steep and rocky descent from the bealach and then the path winds around and

over the low knolls heading in a generally northern direction but contouring round to avoid the worst of the damp ground. The route is particularly boggy as you descend through a small gorge but keep close to the rock wall on your right to avoid the worst of it.

5. Approximately a mile after leaving the Bealach Chruidh the ground flattens out and you reach a metal gate into a fenced area just short of Lochan gun Ghrunnd, the bottomless loch. The path leads across the middle of this very boggy area but it is advisable to turn sharp right from the gate, heading towards a rocky ridge, and follow the edge of this to try and keep your feet dry. After 200 metres you should see the main path joining from your left as you pass near the lochan.

6. Passing the sheepfold and partially ruined shepherd's house on your right, the route heads northwards over a low wire mesh fence and across a flat area of damp grassland where it becomes difficult to see the path. The stone ruins

Shipping traffic crossing through the Caol/ Kyle of Rona with the Torridon hills in the background (NF)

of abandoned croft houses can be seen where, in 1871, there were 12 families living. The hill on Eilean Tigh comes in to view but there is still at least another half mile to go along the side of a stream bed before you reach the beach at Kyle/ Caol Rona.

Meall Mor on Eilean Tigh (TK)

7. If you want to continue on to Eilean Tigh follow a path on your left, uphill though the bracken onto the headland and along to overlook the rocky and slippery causeway across to this tidal island – check tide times and allow yourself no more than 2 hours either side of low tide to cross the causeway. There are some paths on the island but it is really a question of heading for the highest ground with the occasional easy scramble to reach the summit of Meall Mor (111m/ 365 feet). But the view is worth it as you look back south, along the spine of Raasay and across the Kyle to the island of Rona with the hills of Torridon in the distance. This is a very special place combining a sense of wildness and isolation, where about 150 years ago one, and for a short

time, 2 families lived here. There are several caves on the north coast of Eilean Tigh as well as Raasay's most northerly point at Rubha nan Sgarbh.

8. Now retrace your outgoing route and, as you walk through this remote landscape, perhaps think of the children of school age from the north of Raasay 'walking four miles each morning of the academic term down the track from Kyle Rona to Torran School... and then each weekday afternoon they walked four miles back again' (extract from *Calum's Road* by Roger Hutchinson, 2006).

9. As you begin to gain some height after leaving the shore at Kyle Rona you will see a bothy over to your left which is maintained by the Mountain Bothy Association and could be a good base for exploring this area or crossing over to the island of Rona.

View from the summit of Meall Mor on Eilean Tigh looking south (RM)

10. When you arrive back at the Bealach Chruidh you could climb west to the summit of Beinn na h-Iolaire before descending south to join the main track again but maybe that is best left for another day.

11. Continue heading south for Torran at the next path junction to reach the stile and gate. After crossing flat 'pavement' rocks the view opens up to reveal a magnificent panorama across Loch Arnish. About 20 minutes after the Fladday/ Kyle Rona path junction you will arrive at Torran where you turn left onto the main track and back to Arnish.

Additional information kindly provided by Andrew Peter Tallach whose great-grandfather was one of the last residents of Eilean Tigh.

RAASAY EAST COAST ROUTE FROM BROCHEL CASTLE TO FEARNS

START/ FINISH

The route is probably easiest to follow from north to south with a starting point at the car parking area just above Brochel Castle and finishing at the road end car park at Fearns. It is obviously preferable to have access to transport at both ends.

DISTANCE
11K / 7 miles

TIME
6 hours

HIGHEST POINT
233 metres

GRADE/ ADVICE

Difficult. Whilst the beginning and end of this walk are on good tracks the main central part is over challenging ground with some landslips and badly eroded sections, and for one short stretch walkers are forced onto the shoreline rocks. There is also about a half kilometre where the route is badly overgrown with bracken and the path becomes very difficult to follow. So the best time of year to walk this route is between November and June when the bracken has died back. It is also best to avoid very high tides for crossing the section over the shore rocks.

A challenging and beautiful walk on the wild side of the island following an old coastal path through giant rocks and beneath towering sandstone cliffs.

Route

1. From the car parking area above Brochel Castle walk back up the road for 100 metres, past the sheep fank, and you will see a metal gate on the left, just as the road begins to climb uphill. Go through this and follow a narrow path across the felled forest area with fine views southwards along the coastal cliffs. The path descends to meet a broader track coming from your right. Join this and head down to near the shoreline. The track crosses an impressive ravine on a newly built wooden bridge and continues southwards towards the prominence of Candle Rock, part of the cliffs that form the dramatic backdrop to the abandoned township of Screapadal.

Looking south along the east coast of Raasay (DS)

2. Some 40 to 50 minutes after leaving Brochel you will arrive at the stone wall which marks the

edge of the old forest area. Go through the metal gate and onto the faint path crossing grassy slopes below the ruined settlement of North Screapadal,

The cliffs of Creag na Bruaich above the east coast route (BH)

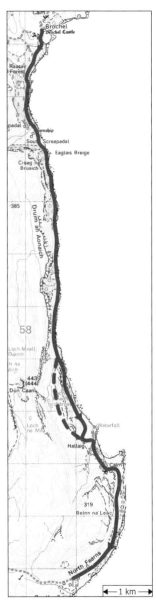

aiming for a tall marker post. This is presumed to be linked to the Royal Navy submarine testing in the Inner Sound between Raasay and Applecross which may also be the reason for the nearby high security wooden shed.

3. The path contours around the grassy slopes beneath Screapadal to lead down to a stream by a tree. You can either make your way up and around the back of it, or cut the corner across some boggy ground to rejoin the track which leads into a birch wood. Cross a gap between large fallen rocks that presumably once formed part of those daunting sandstone cliffs of Creag na Bruaich towering above you. Was that in the Jurassic era or yesterday?

4. The track has now narrowed to a path as the way south opens up and you pass the large shoreline rock of Eaglais Briege, the False Church, some 3 kilometres into the walk. It continues along the grassy foreshore for just over a kilometre, weaving its way between the large rocks and across some fallen trees. The path becomes 'braided' as some

Landslide on the east coast route (BH)

Outline of an angel in the rock (NF)

landslips have necessitated a number of alternative routes to be created. There is a particularly large rock on the seashore, notable partly because of its size and partly because there is an angel here. Yes, a distinct outline of a winged angel is etched in black rock into the paler sandstone.

5. The crux of this route is now reached when you arrive at a headland cliff which has collapsed onto the shoreline rocks, with the original path swept away. It is possible to climb up beside a burn to a holly tree and traverse along sheep tracks well above the shoreline but progress is slow with a tortuous descent back to the main path. So the rather uninviting shoreline rocks are likely to be the best way forward unless there is a particularly high tide.

6. Walk down onto the shore and make your way south, carefully picking your route through the slippery boulders and wave-cut platforms. Keep a

look out for fossils amongst the shattered sedimentary rocks. After about 150 metres the vertical mud cliff at the head of the shore gives way to a steep grassy slope with birch trees and you can scramble up the bank to follow a well-defined sheep track.

7. Continue along this through birch woods, open hillside and rock fall gardens, always in sight of the shore, some 20 to 30 metres above it. There is one mudslide to be negotiated but this can easily be avoided by climbing around the top of it.

8. After about 50 minutes from stepping onto those shore rocks, cross a stream with waterfalls above you and enter a bracken filled giant rock garden. This will be a difficult section to negotiate when the bracken is at its full height during the summer months with the path hidden by the ferns and finding your footing through the rocks particularly hazardous.

The start of the traverse across the shoreline rocks (DS)

9. Once you have escaped from the bracken the path is clear to see as it makes its way on grassy slopes just above the beach towards a prominent sharp pointed hill with a vertical cliff face dropping in to the sea. This appears to guard the shoreline ahead but your route goes just to the right, or west, of this to climb up beside the burn that comes down from Loch a' Chada-charnaich.

Rock formations on the east
coast route (NF)

10. Just over 200 metres up from the shore you
will come to two ruined stone buildings. There is
a metal gate through the fence and you can either
go through this to follow a shoreline, and shorter
route, or continue up to the loch and make your
way around to the top of Hallaig. (The walk from
Fearns to Hallaig describes part of this route.) The
shoreline route is more scenic, as well as shorter, so
it is included in this route.

11. Once through the gate keep to the left to avoid
some boggy ground and in 150 metres follow an
obvious path through the wood and then out onto
open ground for about 200 metres, making your
way gradually down to the shore.

12. There is a fine grassy track close to the shoreline
to follow for about a kilometre, passing a ruined
building at the edge of the beach, before gradually
gaining height to arrive at the large stone-walled
enclosure at Hallaig.

13. Contour round the hillside from the wall on a path that leads down to a burn, which you can easily ford, and then up through the birch trees to meet other tracks that are joining together for the route to Fearns.

14. The path crosses an open grassy area before entering another birch wood and along a terrace above a beautiful curving bay.

Path through the bracken approaching the cliffs of Gualann na Leac and the track to Fearns (RM)

The path narrows and there is a particularly muddy few metres as it bears left to go round the base of those dark cliffs of Gualann na Leac crowding above you. The ruined building which you pass was built to stable the ponies of stalking parties.

15. The full beauty of the bay now opens up as you come to the cairn erected in memory of Sorley MacLean with his poem 'Hallaig' printed in Gaelic and English on the bronze plaque.

16. The last section to Fearns is along a broad grassy track beneath the cliffs. There are fine views across the Inner Sound and south towards the island of Scalpay and the hills of Skye, all the way to the small parking space at the road end in Fearns, just under 3 kilometres from the memorial cairn.

Additional information and route planning kindly provided by Darryl Simpson a keen walker and joint owner, with his wife, Elizabeth, of the Oystercatcher House Bed and Breakfast.

OTHER WALKS

It is possible to combine some of the walks, for instance linking Dun Caan to the ones for Hallaig and Beinn na Leac, or crossing the island from Glam to Screapadal. A popular guide to long distance routes in the north-west of Scotland has an island end-to-end route from Eyre to Kyle Rona described as a two-day backpack trip. Some of the route descriptions do contain suggestions on how walks might be extended but, with the exception of the East Coast traverse, there is no need to have transport at both ends.

It is only a short crossing from the north of Raasay to neighbouring Rona but there are no direct sailing routes between the two islands. Short visits are available on boat trips from Portree and Shieldaig and the island manager of Rona, Bill Cowie (ronalodge@isleofrona.com), may be prepared to ferry small groups across Kyle Rona but you would need to be able to make your way to and from the north of Raasay or stay at the bothy near there. Staying at one of Rona's self-catering houses for a longer visit offers the best chance of walking on the island (www.isleofrona.com).

VISITOR SERVICES

Transport

The ferry terminal at Sconser is a 35 minute drive from the Skye Bridge and there are regular buses from Kyle of Lochalsh to Portree which stop at the Sconser ferry terminal. The spectacular 25 minute ferry journey to the Isle of Raasay must be one of the best value boat trips in the area. At the time of writing there are nine Caledonian MacBrayne ferry sailings each day from Sconser to Raasay, Mondays to Saturdays, in the summer period (April to October). There is a separate winter timetable. The all-year-round Sunday sailings from Sconser are at 10.30 am and 4.30 pm. These timings may change so check the latest schedule by contacting CalMac on 0800-066-5000 or at www. calmac.co.uk. Cars can be brought across to the island (no petrol stations) or left at the car park next to the Sconser ferry terminal. There is no public transport on the island but many of the walks start from the ferry.

Accommodation

Raasay House www.raasay-house.co.uk Tel: 01478-660300
Allt Arais B&B alltarais@supanet.com Tel: 01478-660237
Oystercatcher House B&B www.oystercatcherhousebandb.co.uk Tel: 01478-660277
Self-catering accommodation available at
www.holidaylettings.co.uk/rentals/isle-of-raasay/137274
or www.ownersdirect.co.uk/scotland/SC299.htm

Raasay House

Raasay House offers a range of accommodation, from deluxe to hostel style rooms. There is a cafe-bar and restaurant providing food in a relaxing atmosphere with stunning views over the Sound of Raasay to the Cuillin mountains of Skye. The House is also a base for outdoor adventure, with sessions of sea kayaking, sailing, coasteering and more available to both day visitors and residential guests info@raasay-house.co.uk www.raasay-house. co.uk Tel: 01478 660 300

Raasay Heritage Trust

The Raasay Heritage Trust was formed to promote the language and culture of the island and generate interest in Raasay's literature, history and heritage. A purpose built visitor centre is under construction at Inverarish. For further information about the work of the Heritage Trust and Raasay's history and culture, contact Mrs Rebecca Mackay at 0sgaig@lineone.net or Tel: 01478 660207

Raasay Community Stores and Post Office

Raasay Community Stores and Post Office is situated in the main village of Inverarish, a mile from the ferry terminal and close to several of the walking routes. The licensed shop sells groceries and fresh foods, daily newspapers, local gifts, books and postcards. More information on the latest offers, news and opening time can be found at www.facebook.com/RaasayCommunityStores. Email: Raasaystores@aol.com Tel: 01478 660203

The Silver Grasshopper

The Silver Grasshopper is a local business making hand-made sterling silver jewellery with a jewellery and gift shop (part-time). It is located in The Old Exchange, Clachan, just 5 minutes from the ferry – turn right at the steading building. If the shop is closed contact Fiona on 01478 660232 and for further information look at www.thesilvergrasshopper.com

Further Reading

The following books are available from Raasay Community Stores, Inverarish, as well as from other retail outlets.

Draper, Laurence and Pamela, *The Raasay Iron Mine: Where Enemies Became Friends* (Laurence and Pamela Draper, 1990)
Hutchinson, Roger, *Calum's Road* (Birlinn, 2006)
Savlona, Jim, *A Guide to the Awe-Inspiring Raasay Fissures* (2008)
There is a series of four books entitled 'Every Nook and Cranny' by Rebecca S MacKay – all of which deal with various aspects regarding the place-names of Raasay, Rona, Fladda and Eilean Taighe.

About the Author

Nick Fairweather was born in Sussex in 1945 and brought up in the south of England by his Scottish parents. Childhood holidays in Scotland fostered his love of the hills and since moving to Edinburgh in 1974 he has made his way to the tops of all the Munros and many other hills. He also enjoys cycling and the second edition of his book *Cycling around Scotland*, describing a journey on a mountain bike around the coastline of Scotland, was published by Argyll Publishing in 2010. In the last five years he has been slow cycling across southern Europe in two week sections, from northern Spain through France, Italy and Croatia to Albania and on to Athens. A few years ago he and his wife Dorothy bought a house on Raasay. Nick has been exploring the island ever since.

Praise for *Cycling around Scotland*

'A wonderfully personal and informative book... I was impressed from the first page to the last with all the gems of new information. Enough to get anyone off their sofa and onto the open road' MARK BEAUMONT

'This is a book that should inspire not only cyclists but also anybody with a sense of beauty of Scotland's coastline' ROBIN HARPER

A winter's view of Skye from Raasay (DC)